PROVOKING GOD'S FAVOUR

THE FRAMEWORK OF HOW TRUE BIBLICAL FAVOUR WORKS

by
Oluwole Adekunle

Published By
The Vine Media Communications Ltd

Scripture quotations from The Authorized (King James) Version. Rights in the Authorized Version in the United Kingdom are vested in the Crown. Reproduced by permission of the Crown's patentee, Cambridge University Press

ISBN: 978-0-9574150-2-7

Copyright©2012 by Oluwole Adekunle
Website: www.oluwoleadekunle.com
Twitter: pastorolu1@twitter.com
Facebook: oluwoleadekunle@facebook.com

Published by
The Vine Media Comm. Ltd
T: 078 522 16366
W: www.thevinemedia.co.uk

All rights reserved. No part of this publication may be reproduced, stored in a retrieval system, or transmitted in any form or by any means, mechanical, electronic, photocopying or otherwise without prior written consent of the copyright owner.

Dedication

I dedicate this book to every member of Reality of Grace Ministries International, London for the love and support you have shown to me.

Thank you and God bless.

PROVOKING GOD'S FAVOUR

Acknowledgements

To my lord and Saviour, Jesus Christ: Thank you for entrusting me with this literary treasure. And to all my destiny helpers and ministry partners around the world, thank you for all your support.

Contents

Dedication 3
Acknowledgements 5
Introduction 8

CHAPTER 1 14
The Beauty Of God's Favour

CHAPTER 2 24
The Force Of Knowledge

CHAPTER 3 38
Favour Through Soul Winning

CHAPTER 4 48
The Heart Of Forgiveness

CHAPTER 5 61
Always Speak The Right Words

CHAPTER 6 79
Live Expecting To Be Shown Favour

CHAPTER 7 87
The Beauty Of Humility

CHAPTER 8 97
The Praise Dimension

CHAPTER 9 110
The Force Of Loyalty

CHAPTER 10 121
Favour Is A Seed

CHAPTER 11 132
Releasing Favour By Warfare

CHAPTER 12 142
The Force Of Hardwork

CHAPTER 13 149
Love, The Greatest Of All

Introduction

To enable us to enjoy the best that God has prepared for us in redemption, we have to be more responsible for our actions as members of the body of the Lord Jesus Christ. I know some of us 21st-century preachers have not helped matters by presenting a one-sided gospel that succeeding in life is an all God affair, without balancing that with the roles we have to play too. On the other hand, there's a second group of people who think that succeeding in life is all about how much effort a person puts into his work. Both are partially right, because a false balance is an abomination to God – Proverbs 11:1. It is neither an all man nor an all God affair. For this reason I am writing this book to explore how we need both our inputs plus God's help to enjoy the fullness of God's blessings.

If favour just happens without our own inputs, as some claim, how come things do not change for us unless we attempt to change them?

Introduction

How come we have an untold number of frustrated Christians today who don't know where they are headed? The mere fact that God has clearly stated that without knowledge His own people are susceptible to destruction is enough proof that our inputs to the issues of life are undeniable. Now, it is still not enough to stop at knowledge acquisition, you need to thoroughly apply that knowledge to yourself to enjoy the benefits. I make bold to add that God's people are not just destroyed for lack of knowledge but also for the lack of self-application of the knowledge they have acquired.

> I make bold to add that God's people are not just destroyed for lack of knowledge but also for the lack of self-application of the knowledge they have acquired.

In other words, if Isaac Newton's first law of motion states that everything continues in a state of rest or uniform motion in a straight line unless compelled by some external force to act otherwise, it implies that we must do some things even as Christians in order to create our desired expectations. Must science beat the Bible to it? Must scientists beat the Saints of God to it?

I have to say all this because some self-acclaimed Bible scholars may conclude too quickly that I am implying that favour can be earned through works. No man can earn anything from God on the platform of self-righteousness, but we certainly can on the platform of our faith linked to Him. And we cannot mention the issue of faith without works being added to it, which implies from our simple spiritual equation that it is faith plus works that equals our expected desire. No one can buy a blessing, but you can obey your way into enjoying the blessings you want to the fullest.

A few days ago, a sister called to tell me of her new resolution by the grace of God not to be quick to criticise people any more. When I asked why, she told me that both from a Biblical perspective and practical experience she had seen that it pays to be meek and gentle, because things seem to go well for people with such

> No man can earn anything from God on the platform of self-righteousness, but we certainly can on the platform of our faith linked to Him.

> No one can buy a blessing, but you can obey your way into enjoying the blessings you want to the fullest.

character traits. This was her conclusion, "The bible isn't lying by saying that the meek shall inherit the earth."

There are millions of people going through stuff in their marriages, careers, businesses, ministries and so on who are throwing bombs at the devil for their woes, but who would never give the slightest thought to the fact that though the devil is bad, he shouldn't always be made to carry the blame for our own lapses and foolishness. I had an occasion to present the gospel to two white Britons who came to help us do some work on our church altar, but they wouldn't consider it because their parents never trained them to be church goers. The amazing thing one of them told us was that he wouldn't blame himself but Adam and Eve, who plunged humanity into the mess we are in today. I agree that Adam and Eve blew the fuse, but what are we doing to bring back the light of God's glory into our lives? If they blew the fuse, then we should reconnect the wires and enjoy the light and life that Christ has brought to us. Now, will God agree with them and open the gates of heaven to them when they die if they refuse to accept Jesus in their lifetime? I don't think so, from what the Bible clearly says.

I learnt a lesson from Dr Fredrick K.C. Price's book

> A lot of us know what we have to do to enjoy the best God has for us, but we never do anything about it.

How Faith Works. A man was diagnosed as suffering from malnutrition and needed to eat within thirty minutes or he would die. The man kept telling everyone who paid him a visit that the doctor said that if he didn't eat within thirty minutes he would die. But he didn't eat before the thirty minutes had elapsed and he gave up the ghost. This is exactly what this book is out to correct: a lot of us know what we have to do to enjoy the best God has for us, but we never do anything about it. Does this also remind you of the sons of the prophets who knew that God was going to take up Elijah but only stood to watch the event and never benefited from it? Who said that they couldn't desire a portion of the anointing of the prophet who was about to exit the earth? They knew the will of God, talked about it, but never benefited from it because they didn't know any better how to do something with the information at their disposal.

This book will by the grace of God catapult you to a new level of God's favour in your life in Jesus' name - amen! Please always remember that life will not give you what you deserve, you are to demand from life what you think you deserve. If you wait on life to do what is right, you will live all your life in utter regret.

We shall by the grace of God be exploring the things that cause the favour of God to materialise. We are already favoured, but there are things that make the favour manifest. The fact that a man has a billion dollars in the bank does not mean that he has money to display all the time. To withdraw money, he has to write a cheque for it. If his signature is wrong when he tries to cash the cheque, even though the money belongs to him, no cashier who still loves his or her job will honour the cheque with the irregular signature. Even if he has to use a debit or credit card, he still has to know his pin number to make withdrawals. This is the connection: even though we have been blessed and highly favoured, there are other things required to bring that favour into our lives. We need more than the mere confession of it. The truth of God's word is all encompassing; it is precept upon precept, line upon line. Open your hearts and let us humbly explore together what God by His grace has for us.

> Please always remember that life will not give you what you deserve, you are to demand from life what you think you deserve.

CHAPTER ONE

The Beauty Of God's Favour

Every regenerated covenant child of God is, potentially, a favoured person. This is because he has been translated from the kingdom of darkness to the kingdom of the light of God's Son. A redeemed man ceases to be under the authority of darkness where weeping and gnashing of teeth is the perpetual order (for every subject still in the grip of Satan).

He is now an heir and joint heir to all the riches of Christ. He is automatically raised to the enviable position of an Ambassador of the Lord Jesus Christ, a high representative of the kingdom of God everywhere he shows up on earth. He is not just an Ambassador of Christ on earth, he is also seated with Christ in heavenly places, far above all defeated principalities, powers, rulers of the darkness of this world and defeated wicked spirits in the heavenly places, with an irrevocable decree from the Most High God that no weapon fashioned against him should ever prosper in his walk with God.

Chapter One: The Beauty Of God's Favour

The redeemed man has a heritage of long life and prosperity. He is made and destined to be fruitful in body, very sound in mind and a superman in spirit. No form of barrenness is ever to be his lot. He has been empowered to prosper in whatever he lays his hands to do as long as he walks in the full counsel of God. He is blessed in his going out and his coming in and honoured with a mark placed on him by God that everyone should satisfy him with favour wherever he appears.

> The redeemed man has a heritage of long life and prosperity. He is made and destined to be fruitful in body, very sound in mind and a superman in spirit.

He is raised above every curse because no enchantment or divination is allowed to work against him. The regenerated man has covenant immunity against curses; no one can curse him because he is already blessed of God with all spiritual blessings in heavenly places. Who dares curse the one whom God has blessed? The wife of his youth should be the wife of his old age; no one is permitted by God to put them asunder, whether with legislative or judicial power. He should enjoy peace and God's deliverance, no matter the fierceness of the opposition against him from Satan and his defeated foes.

The joy of the Lord should be his strength every waking morning. He is not to lack wisdom, understanding and direction in all the affairs of his life. His physical and spiritual strength should not abate; they should increase as his days here on earth increase. The list of his blessings is an endless one. What a redemption we have in Christ Jesus!

WRONG ASSUMPTIONS ABOUT HOW FAVOUR WORKS

If we must be truthful to each other as Saints of God and His Christ, we will agree that an average covenant child of God hardly experiences a quarter of all these goodies listed. The simple reason is that we have taken the benevolence of favour as a substitute for laziness. We forget that covenant promises demand conscious self-application

> We forget that covenant promises demand conscious self-application to work them out. None of the good promises of God ever works by wishful thinking; the necessary steps have to be taken to activate each of them to produce for us.

to work them out. None of the good promises of God ever works by wishful thinking; the necessary steps have to be taken to activate each of them to produce for us. As passionate as God was to let go His only begotten Son to die for the sins of the whole world, no one's salvation materialises unless, of course, he accepts and confesses Jesus Christ as Saviour and Lord. Failure to do that ends the person's life in hell where he/she will burn night and day for ever. The natural human mind will refute the fact that failure to receive the Person of Jesus Christ as Saviour and Lord ends a man's life in eternal damnation, without realising that sentimentality and spirituality are in most cases diametrically opposed to each other. The Bible has clearly stated this: <u>"I tell you, Nay: except ye repent, ye shall all likewise perish" Luke 13:3.</u> This is repeated in verse 5 of Luke 13.

Favour does not work automatically, whether with God or with man. Things must be done to set it in motion. We have those who never give help to people in difficulty, yet when they have problems themselves, they expect help from every quarter possible. How reasonable and just is that? Some attack the message of prosperity like a plague, not because they hate to be rich but for the covenant demands of tithes and offerings to which they find it difficult to submit.

For some, the "grace" to forgive is all they need so that the heaven of brass over them can be removed in order that the rain of favour may fall; but they will never give in to this grace just because they feel too big to be hurt by anyone. Sometimes failure to forgive, in a way, reveals that we still have innate pride to deal with. We are the ones making it appear as if God is a liar before the heathen. This is because He has not really appeared to be who we profess Him to be due to our gross inconsistencies in following His instructions for us. God is not a liar! If you have anything against your neighbour and you want your prayers answered by any means, the remedy is not to add fasting to your prayers in order to move God. Just forgive and heaven will open up unto you. If you are finding this difficult to do, call for help from your pastor or an elder you respect. The transgressor will always think that self-affliction is the way out in difficult times, while in fact it is simple obedience he needs.

Proverbs 13:15
Good understanding giveth favour: but the way of the transgressors is hard.

Chapter One: The Beauty Of God's Favour

Some walk in pride and want God to promote them by all means. Every one of God's promises has one condition or another attached to it - which we deliberately disobey in most cases. The mercy of God is not a licence to carry on with presumptuous sins (Romans 6:1). Christians need not make sin a habit, even though we all know that we are only working towards perfection or spiritual maturity each day. God will only favour us according to His Word and not outside of it, no matter how much we ceaselessly hallow His name because of our desperation to be favoured. God never works outside His will.

You may speak in tongues for twelve hours every day because you want God to favour you with a second wife while the first is still alive. My brother, He will not do it. Some people will go into fasting and prayer so as not to be caught in their drug trafficking business. This is how far some have degenerated in the church of Jesus Christ today. That your pastor has not been bold enough to tell you does not make it right. If you have tried this in the past and you were not caught, count yourself lucky and quickly repent and forsake the business without a second thought. If you don't, the devil is setting you up for life imprisonment or the death penalty, depending on the law in operation wherever you finally get caught. So beware!

In this book, mercy, grace and favour are used interchangeably as they practically mean the same thing. The two scriptures below will help throw more light on what I want to pass across to the precious Saints of God.

> *Psalm 119:58 (emphasis mine)*
> *I entreated thy favour with my whole heart: be merciful unto me <u>according to thy word.</u>*

> *Psalms 119:41 (emphasis mine)*
> *Let thy mercies come also unto me, O LORD, even thy salvation, <u>according to thy word</u>.*

> God will only favour you within the confines of His will, never outside of it.

The mercies of God mentioned in the two verses above, in David's opinion by the Holy Spirit, are according to the word of God – that is, His standard for living. God will only favour you within the confines of His will, never outside of it. And you have to walk in His will to enjoy it. In other words, favour only comes in accordance with the Word. God favours you with goodies that are within the confines of His word. A wise man should seek what provokes God's favour and not the favour itself.

Because God wants us to enjoy His favour to the fullest, He has given each one of us the ability to know the mysteries of the kingdom. This He ensured by giving us His Holy Spirit, the great Teacher - Mark 4:11. The same Holy Spirit comes to let us know the things that are freely given to us by God - 1 Corinthians 2:12. Most of the things He tells us might not be in agreement with our preconceived personal philosophy or the lifestyle we have adopted from the world. Our responsibility is to be open to Him.

Our yieldedness to Him should cause us to follow Him foolishly. Is it not a foolish thing to give away some of what you have in order to have more? The world's system teaches that you get richer the more you are able to hoard what you have and try, as much as possible, to get what others have in addition to yours. Locating a vision for living is also a very foolish act to many people, especially when you have to forsake a career you have spent so much time developing to pursue another path entirely. People just do not understand why someone who read medicine would forsake it just because he has discovered that he should be a musician.

One time Peter struggled all night long and could not catch any fish; all his techniques failed him and none of his earlier training helped him at all. In frustration, he packed up his fishing nets and began to wash them in utter surrender to the hopelessness that characterised his experience. He had not finished washing his nets when Jesus, the One with the answer to every question, appeared on the scene. He borrowed Peter's boat for His crusade and thereafter commanded Peter to launch back into the deep for a huge catch. Peter hesitated a little and tried explaining all his futile efforts, made acute by an unnatural occurrence. There had been no fish in sight during the night when they naturally come out. Since he thought he had nothing to lose afterwards, he finally bowed to the authority of Jesus' command. "We have toiled all night and caught nothing, but nevertheless at your word, I will let down the net," he said. He had the greatest catch of his life that morning because he responded to a supposedly "stupid" but divine command. What provoked that favour was his obedience.

Jesus may not be with you physically today, but the Word of God, the Bible, is there for you to obey, because

Chapter One: The Beauty Of God's Favour

He is the same yesterday, and today and for ever. You can be sure that He will never deny you your expected result in any area where you stretch yourself to obey Him.

Mary, the biological mother of our Lord Jesus Christ, definitely could not have been the only virgin on earth when God sought a womb to carry His son. Her simple act of obedience in believing that a woman could conceive supernaturally, without meeting a man, gave her that privilege. The angel Gabriel told her that she had found favour with God, possibly because she had been obedient to the commandments of God in the past.

This book will further enlighten us on the little things that we neglect but that, when obeyed, will cause the doors of heaven to be perpetually opened to us. While nobody can lay claim to knowing all things (I Corinthians 8:2), it is my earnest prayer that the Holy Spirit will expound this truth beyond all you will read in the pages of this book.

CHAPTER TWO

The Force Of Knowledge

Knowledge is the sole determinant of the degree of favour a man enjoys in life. This is because in most cases, how much you know is how much you are known in any field of endeavour. Lionel Messi is a world-class footballer today and, of course, about the most popular because of his undeniable mastery of the round leather ball. Mention Usain Bolt and athletics quickly comes to mind. You cannot say Michael Schumacher and not immediately register Formula One car racing. All these superstars are all very good in their chosen careers and we can see the tremendous favour they enjoy by way of the money they are paid through adverts, endorsements and all other channels. No good business strategist will use a mediocre person for an advert, because people want to be associated only with those who are successful.

> No good business strategist will use a mediocre person for an advert, because people want to be associated only with those who are successful.

Chapter Two: The Force Of Knowledge

And what I have discovered to be the main secret of the success of these men is what I mentioned earlier - a good knowledge of what they have chosen to do for a living. The seed that fell on the good ground in the parable of the sower in Mark chapter 4 brought forth thirty-, sixty- and a hundredfold returns. Your percentage yield is determined by how much insight you have gained in the subject matter you are exploring (that is, how much attention you give to the Word in a particular area). That is why some people may be very rich materially and yet deficient in marital issues. This is simply because they have not given detailed attention to the issue of marriage as compared to the amount they have given to prosperity. The Word of God's power upholds all things. Mark the word "all". In other words, there is nothing to which the Word has no answer. But answers to the questions of our life will only come through a diligent search for the truth.

For instance, this book on favour is a revelation of how much attention I have given to the subject. I don't joke about the subject of favour at all. I cannot get tired of listening to tapes and reading books on it, because I have discovered that success in life is not based on your age, the colour of your skin or eyes or the class of your degree. Favour is the referee that determines the outcome of all

> Favour is the referee that determines the outcome of all the issues of life. But the truth is that to unlock favour, the knowledge of what makes it work must be understood.

the issues of life. But the truth is that to unlock favour, the knowledge of what makes it work must be understood. The deeper one's insight into the subject of favour is, the more the manifestation of it in one's life. I am writing this book based on the insight I have gained. In other words, someone with a deeper insight than me will definitely enjoy more manifestation of favour.

1 Corinthians 15:10
But by the grace of God I am what I am: and his grace which was bestowed upon me was not in vain; but I laboured more abundantly than they all: yet not I, but the grace of God which was with me.

The heighted Bible verse above was a statement made by Apostle Paul. He revealed, through the inspiration of the Holy Spirit, that grace (or favour) determines a man's status. But for that status to be progressively altered positively, you have to increase in knowledge. Knowledge determines favour/grace, while grace determines placement. We can conclude therefore that knowledge ultimately determines status. The more knowledge you have, the more colour is added to your life. Another way of putting it is that more knowledge translates into more beauty.

> Knowledge determines favour/grace, while grace determines placement.

A junior worker who was dreaded by almost every other worker - both senior and junior - had threatened to deal with me spiritually because I ordered that he should be questioned for refusing to obey my team leader's orders. All I said was, "Let God punish me if I ever make your threat a prayer point when I get home." This statement may not be totally acceptable to you, but that was the exact thing I said out of holy anger. He had said openly that it was all over with me and that I was going to feel his weight spiritually. He actually made attempts on my life, but he failed woefully. He had forgotten that his father, the devil, is less than a featherweight that has been reduced to ashes under the soles of the feet of the Saints of God.

> If I have been delivered from Satan, I don't need to have sleepless nights over one of his subjects.

My grace to overcome was based on insight. For me it was not the time to start running from pillar to post to seek spiritual help. I saved that time and didn't lose a second's sleep. The reason is simple: I knew too well that his threat came two thousand years too late; I have already been delivered from the authority of darkness. If I have been delivered from Satan, I don't need to have sleepless nights over one of his subjects. I was very aware that I am eternally seated with Christ in heavenly places far above the demons that were to put his diabolical plans into effect. I am still seated far above him even now. I mean every single word I am saying. I know too well that my life is hidden in Christ with God and that whatever is kept in His care is safe and secure. I know too well that no counsel can work against the ones God has hidden (Psalm 83:3). I know too well that no one can curse the ones God has blessed and, praise God, I am blessed with all spiritual blessings in Christ (Num. 23:8; Eph. 1:3). I know too well that Jesus has paralysed all principalities, powers, dominions and thrones and has made an open show of them all (Col. 2:15). I was the one Christ displayed before all the demoniacal forces as freed, blessed, prosperous, forgiven, cleansed and seated with Him in heavenly places. Praise God! All these produced the grace or favour for my victory.

> *Psalm 41:11*
> *By this I know that thou favourest me, because mine enemy doth not triumph over me.*

I provoked God's favour for my deliverance over the threat of that Satanist because I knew that I was God's favoured person for victory. Mind you, the victory was not assumed but has been searched out and continually and firmly declared for my justification. That was why I didn't see the need to lose any sleep. Do you know that deliverance is a proof of the presence of God's favour upon any life? Now in the new birth, is there any one who is not or has not been favoured by God? But until the average

> Now in the new birth, is there any one who is not or has not been favoured by God? But until the average Christian wakes up to the fact that it is knowledge that brings the beauty of redemption, we will still be far from all that redemption has to offer.

Christian wakes up to the fact that it is knowledge that brings the beauty of redemption, we will still be far from all that redemption has to offer.

> Every revelation of or illumination into the Word precedes the problem God has foreseen and revealed it to solve.

Let me give you a piece of advice that will be of immense benefit: don't wait for a problem to surface before you begin to search the Word for your declaration of victory over Satan and his works. Every revelation of or illumination into the Word precedes the problem God has foreseen and revealed it to solve. So keep declaring the revealed Word before the problem surfaces. This is bound to make your victory a cheap one when you finally confront the issue. Learn a lesson from professional boxers: they have sparring partners with whom they fight to enable them to keep fit, so that they aren't rusty when the true championship bout arrives.

2 Peter 1:2-4
Grace and peace be multiplied unto you through the knowledge of God, and of Jesus our Lord, according as his divine power hath given us all that pertain to

life and godliness, through the knowledge of him that hath called us to glory and virtue: whereby are given unto us exceeding great and precious promises: that by these ye might be partakers of the divine nature, having escaped the corruption that is in the world through lust.

Do you know that most Christians cannot quote twenty promises at a go? It is unthinkable that one lacks competence in what is supposed to make us exceed and be great in life, what should make us look like God or produce naturally like God.

Now, can a snake bite kill God? You can now begin to see why Apostle Paul made a mess of the venomous viper that bit him on the island of Malta. Those who witnessed the scene were waiting for him to die from the snake bite, but they all waited in vain. Buried in Paul's spirit was the truth that no weapon formed against him would prosper; that nothing should by any means hurt him; that he would drink deadly poison and it would not hurt him. What was loaded into his spirit sustained him. Halleluiah!

Israel would never have returned from the land of

Babylon if Daniel didn't research to find out that they were to spend not more than seventy years in captivity. But the same was not true for the children of Israel in the land of Egypt. They were to spend four hundred years in captivity, although they ended up spending four hundred and thirty years. Where did the extra thirty years come from? Was it that God didn't remember the stipulated time for freedom? From Daniel's research we can conclude that no one bothered to find out how long they were to be there. God probably prompted Moses ten years before the time to organise the exodus, but the man in his perfect humanity thought that the release of Israel was to be done by punches. Because Moses didn't understand how he was to lead the people, he got himself into trouble and ran into exile when his carnal method failed him. He killed an Egyptian who maltreated a Hebrew and the case was leaked later, so he had to escape to preserve his life. He spent an unplanned forty years in exile and therefore caused the thirty years extra that Israel spent before its victory was secured. His labour wearied many people because he didn't know how to lead the

> The prophecy that you don't work out accurately will not produce no matter how profound the Prophet who prophesied it.

people of God into their promised city. The prophecy that you don't work out accurately will not produce no matter how profound the Prophet who prophesied it.

Ecclesiastes 10:15
The labour of the foolish wearieth every one of them, because he knoweth not how to go to the city.

The healing favour has been established for over two thousand years now, but whom do we blame for some still seeing healing as a thing to be enjoyed in the future? It is not "I will be healed" but "I have been healed". When church folks come with a health issue, the first thing I try to drill into them is that they are not sick trying to be healed, but that they are already made whole by the stripes of Jesus fighting not to be sick. We are to stand in the liberty wherewith Christ has made us whole to fight. You are not standing on your liberty when you accept that you are sick (Gal. 5:1). This is because by the stripes of Jesus we have been made completely whole (1 Peter 2:24). People claim to have seen Jesus and to have received promises from Him to heal and raise them from their sick beds in the course of their sickness. I am not here to disprove their divine experiences or visitations, but I think Jesus would have meant that He would make manifest the profit of the stripes on His body, put there by the cruel Roman soldiers' whips in a bid to guarantee their healing. He was brutally beaten to guarantee our healing. Thank God for *The Passion of the Christ* by Mel Gibson, which was a close revelation of what He suffered. He will never hang on any cross again – for ever and ever - because afflictions will never arise a second time (Nahum 1:9). He must have meant, "My finished work, when I was beaten, would be made manifest." This is because, spiritually or legally, our healing has been totally paid for already. The favour of healing has been wrought already, but some church folks can't wait for "the day Jesus will heal them". What an irony! The favours of deliverance and perfect health are all in the past tense.

The Ethiopian eunuch came face to face with salvation, but because of lack of understanding he would have missed the great message on the page he was reading when Philip met him. He would have died and gone to hell if the action to be taken for salvation (to be made manifest) had not been taken. Thank God for the angel of the Lord who transported Philip mysteriously to the eunuch's side to aid him. The same Philip connection can be enjoyed today through the purchase of the anointed tapes and books of men of God. That you were not in a particular programme or conference when it was held should not mean that you can't be a beneficiary of all that God did for those who were present. If the Holy Spirit allows the tapes into your hands, it is like the miraculous transportation of Philip to the side of the Ethiopian eunuch to grant him a deeper understanding in the area in which God wanted to effect salvation in him. Are you sure that this book is not a Philip by your side on your wilderness of ill luck, defeat, stagnation, shame and reproach in some areas of your life? Are you sure that this book is not sent to ask you, "understandeth thou how favour works?" (Acts 8: 30).

GO ALL OUT FOR KNOWLEDGE

Knowledge is power. Go for it. How much you know guarantees how much you are known; go after knowledge. How much you learn guarantees how much you earn; go after knowledge. Readers are leaders, they say. Therefore, go after knowledge. Knowledge gives birth to confidence and eliminates, or at least eases, the burdens of life.

Some people will never invest because of fear. They are afraid because they do not know that a thorough knowledge of what they want to invest in reduces the risk of failure.

> If your mind is not renewed in the knowledge of God's word, you cannot be renowned in God's kingdom.

If your mind is not renewed in the knowledge of God's word, you cannot be renowned in God's kingdom. Therefore, go after knowledge. 1 Samuel 2:3b tells us that God is a God of knowledge; therefore in order to look like Him, we must be children of knowledge too. If the pains of knowledge acquisition weigh ounces, the pains of ignorance weigh tons. Everybody likes what is good, but we forget the truth of God's word that a soul without knowledge is not good (Proverbs 19:2). That means that a life without knowledge is a bad life. Get knowledge and save your children from the curse on the children of the ignorant (Hosea 4:6).

> If the pains of knowledge acquisition weigh ounces, the pains of ignorance weigh tons.

Do you know that ignorance gets people ignored? Yet people will rather be bitter about those who ignored them than take a look to see why they were ignored in the first place. Who will give you any recognition in your field of endeavour if you are not a man given to books in that field? There is nobody. In other words, you cannot boo a man in his field of endeavour when he is given to books in it.

CHAPTER THREE

Favour Through Soul Winning

We, the body of Christ, have become very complacent about the great commission of soul winning. We have become a "name it and claim it" society. We now major on the minor things of life and minor on the major things that make life worth living.

The Saints of God would fast for thirty days and more only if it would produce a better job, buy a new car, build a house or achieve for them a great height in the mundane things of the world. Are all these things bad in themselves? Absolutely not! It is only a question of misplaced priority. No longer will the church fast and pray fervently for strongholds holding people back from serving God to be broken. Instead it's all about abundance - which in a very real sense is not being experienced in magnitudes commensurate with the efforts and resources poured into global junketing to attend unending conferences and seminars. I am definitely not against prosperity, but I am against the way preachers preach it without balancing things up.

> *Proverbs 11:1*
> *A false balance is an abomination to the LORD: but a just weight is his delight.*

Preachers these days will go all out to raise money but do very little to heal the sick. They can easily chicken out of doing this with claims that they have not been anointed to heal. Preachers simply don't want to fast any more. No wonder that Jesus asked whether He will find faith on earth when He comes back. In the context in which He said that in Luke 18, He meant whether He would still find rugged men who would not take "no" for an answer when confronted with stubborn problems. The emphasis there was not that of the faith that comes by hearing the word of God, but the faith that never says no to oppositions; the faith that is ready to do everything necessary to produce what is desired. Read from verse one of Luke 18 to get the whole story.

We sow much and reap very little, if there is anything to reap at all, because we refuse to heed the

> Evangelism is foremost on God's agenda after worship and closest to His heart.

admonishment to consider our ways (Haggai 1:6-7). Evangelism is foremost on God's agenda after worship and closest to His heart. We cannot shy away from this truth. The purpose of wealth, in the first place, is to get the gospel preached across the cities of the world (Zechariah 1:17). We are first and foremost to expand the kingdom of God and not to boost our lust for carnal things.

Matthew 6:33
But seek ye first the kingdom of God, and his righteousness; and all these things shall be added unto you.

Seeking first the kingdom of God and his righteousness provokes God's favour more than anything. We must realise that God has a need too. His most precious creatures, made in His image and likeness, are dying en masse on a daily basis and are making hell their permanent abode. It is never His will that the devil should deceive them and blind their minds from seeing Jesus Christ of Nazareth as the only sacrifice for every man's sin. The world must be reconciled to God. God has given us that ministry to reconcile sinners to Him, not to impute their sins against them. We are the ones to carry out this awareness campaign.

II Corinthians 5:19
To wit, that God was in Christ, reconciling the world unto himself, not imputing their trespasses unto them; and hath committed unto us the word of reconciliation.

The early church swam in great favour both with God and men (Acts 2:46-47), because Christ, the burden Remover and yoke Destroyer, was their core message. Soul winning was their passion, not fund raising.

You can start functioning in the place of your assignment today by shedding your indifference and bad attitude towards that alcoholic neighbour whom you have been avoiding, just for the sake of winning him to Christ. Everything God would ever do to save him has been accomplished already in Christ's death and resurrection. Our duty is to cause him to see the love of God, which the devil has blinded his mind from seeing (II Corinthians 4:4). We are not to win the dying world

> We are not to win the dying world through our own eloquence of speech or by mounting pressure on them, but by our total dependence on the Holy Spirit to speak through us to convince them of sin and of the judgement to come.

through our own eloquence of speech or by mounting pressure on them, but by our total dependence on the Holy Spirit to speak through us to convince them of sin and of the judgement to come.

The average sinner is already condemned as long as he refuses the Lordship of Christ, so don't go and tell him what he already knows. Instead, tell him that the eternal death sentence is reversible as long as he is still alive. Let him know that by simply accepting Jesus Christ as Lord and Saviour, believing it in his heart and confessing it with his mouth, the new birth is imparted into him instantly, thereby making him a brand new creature.

Romans 10: 9-10
That if thou shalt confess with the mouth the Lord Jesus, and shalt believe in thine heart that God hath raised him from the dead, thou shalt be saved. For

with the heart man believeth unto righteousness; and with the mouth confession is made unto salvation.

We are the salt of the earth. We must mix with sinners with the good intention of influencing them positively for God. If, however, we find out that the reverse is becoming the case in our association with them, then we have to quickly retrace our steps. Please, heed this advice, because I know what dimensions unguarded associations can take on. The faith of many sincere brothers has been infected because they allowed their lust to draw them to witness to the wrong people. Don't use the guise of evangelism to fulfil your ungodly desires for beautiful women or handsome men. Be warned! Do you know that some men will not preach to anyone except women? And not just any kind of woman, but the very pretty type. The same applies to some women whose evangelistic fervour is directed only at six-foot men with the latest cars. Who are we deceiving? Be careful not to fulfil your lustful desires in the guise of soul winning. You don't need anyone to mess you up because you want him to receive Jesus; Jesus has been messed up enough for the sins of the whole world. We should not isolate ourselves, but must insulate ourselves when we come into close contact with those who can influence us negatively.

I have boarded cabs I ended not paying for, in a place like London, because I led the cab driver to Christ as we went on the journey. This has happened on several occasions. The intention was never to evade the payment of my transport fares. As a matter of fact, I came across some who never gave the slightest attention to what I had to say to them about Christ, either because they were Muslims, occultists or just people who are indifferent to religious matters. I give that example as proof that evangelism done in truth and spirit can provoke God's favour on the spot.

If you are favourably disposed to the fulfilment of God's purpose on earth, then you can boldly declare that God's abundant prosperity is your portion.

Psalms 35:27
Let them shout for joy, and be glad, that favour my righteous cause: yea, let them say continually, let the LORD be magnified, which hath pleasure in the prosperity of his servant.

The preaching of the gospel does not make people societal rejects, as the devil would love us to believe. Rather, it provides a platform for God to make one a star on earth. A total commitment to evangelism unlocks God's grace upon people. Needs are met supernaturally in the most inexplicable ways.

> **The preaching of the gospel does not make people societal rejects, as the devil would love us to believe. Rather, it provides a platform for God to make one a star on earth.**

Daniel 12:3
And they that be wise shall shine as the brightness of the firmament; and they that turn many to righteousness as the stars for ever and ever.

In Proverbs 11:30, wise men were defined as soul winners; therefore a soul winner who continually turns people to righteousness cannot but shine here on earth, as we can read in the verse given above.

Let us see what Jesus Himself had to say about those who are ready to deny themselves in this world in order to further His work.

Mark 10:29-30
And Jesus answered and said, Verily I say unto you, There is no man that hath left house, or brethren, or sisters, or father, or mother, or wife, or children, or lands, for my sake and the gospels', But he shall receive a hundredfold now in this time, houses, and brethren, and sisters, and mothers, and children, and lands, with persecutions; and in the world to come eternal life.

People are leaving their jobs today to answer the call of God; some have relocated outside the shores of their countries in response to the Macedonian call. Initially things will always appear very tough and unpleasant, judging from the lifestyle you abandoned. But from the passage above, things are not bound to remain that way, they must, by the faithfulness of the One who has given His Word, change for the better. Not when we get to heaven, but right here on earth! Read the scriptural quotation again. It is NOW, in this time.

The only thing I must not fail to include is that you must make sure your sacrifices are for the sake of Christ and the gospel and not because you want a wife or a husband, or that you want to be elected a deacon or to get yourself a job. If the priority is right, then the hundredfold returns await you. Never mind the persecutions attached. People will naturally envy a prosperous man and wish the worst for him. I think it is better to be persecuted as a very successful and favoured man than celebrated as a worthless pauper. There is joy in heaven over one soul that gets saved. You cannot create joy in heaven and God will not reward you by creating joy for you here on earth. This is one way to swim in God's favour.

> I think it is better to be persecuted as a very successful and favoured man than celebrated as a worthless pauper.

CHAPTER FOUR

The Heart Of Forgiveness

I have discovered from scriptures by the help of the Holy Spirit that having a tender heart of forgiveness provokes God's favour. It was the common denominator that attracted the favour of God to some notable Bible characters. A Father with very deep thoughts such as our God would not just do something for anybody without having His reasons. He doesn't act just because He has the power to do all things. He reasons very deeply. So we know that He doesn't act randomly, since actions are very often the products of our thoughts (Isaiah 1: 18-19).

God does His things righteously. That is why He is called a just God. For a Holy God to single out someone for greatness and leave others as societal rejects would be nothing but a miscarriage of justice.

> For a Holy God to single out someone for greatness and leave others as societal rejects would be nothing but a miscarriage of justice.

He does not hand pick people to favour, His favourites are those who do His will. Isn't it the joy of every responsible earthly father to see to it that all his children fare very well? In fact, extra care is given to those who are not doing well so that they can catch up. If your child is performing poorly in school, won't you hire a tutor for him if you have the means? How much more would this apply to a good God like ours. He passionately desires to favour us, but He has His modus operandi. God is no respecter of persons, but He does respects principles when those principles are products of His own thoughts.

> God is no respecter of persons, but He does respects principles when those principles are products of His own thoughts.

Every man is the architect of his own fortune or misfortune. For instance, if a man pins another man down in a brawl, refusing to let him go, he has to stay with the one he is pinning down. In the event of a bomb alert in that neighbourhood, if he refuses to let go of the other

> Every man is the architect of his own fortune or misfortune.

> We must always remember that lack of forgiveness stagnates.

man and run for dear life, the two of them would die there if the bomb eventually exploded. The bomb would kill the two of them. So many people have hindered their own blessings because they just would not let go to let God. Why die before your time because of anger when you have the choice of a long life? We must always remember that lack of forgiveness stagnates.

Job 5:2
For wrath killeth the foolish man, and envy slayeth the silly one.

> You are only helping yourself when you forgive, because you are the one carrying the burden of bitterness everywhere you go.

Even if you insist on not letting the man go and you drag him along with you in a bid to make progress at all costs, you can be sure that you'll get tired and worn out in no time because of your "extra luggage". You are only helping yourself when you forgive, because you are the one carrying the burden of bitterness everywhere you go. The irony of the whole thing is that the person you are begrudging may not even be aware of it in the first place. I repeat once more, kindly let go of every offence and let God.

We offend people too, don't we? Most of us want justice at all costs when we are sinned against, but we cry for mercy when we sin against someone else. Is that just? What you sow is what you will reap, no matter how highly placed you are in the kingdom's work. Remember, the first three words of Gal 6:7 are "Be not deceived...." So deception has a serious role to play in this issue. Don't be deceived that you've been born again for thirty- five years now or that you gave the highest donation when you were building your last auditorium. Don't be deceived that you were the one who brought revival to your nation and so on. So many things make us think that we can be excused of some basic Biblical principles. The truth is that God's word is not unilateral. It is all encompassing from Genesis to Revelation, from the Law to the Prophets and to the new covenant in Christ.

This life is so short that we do not really need all the stress we go

> This life is so short that we do not really need all the stress we go through each day.

through each day. Some people are malicious today because someone they consider too junior to them refused to greet them the last time they met at their town meeting or old boys' alumni get-together. If such meetings hinder the flow of God's grace and peace in your life, then it is high time you avoid them. And if you so love to be greeted respectfully, then try as much as possible to greet yourself very well every morning when you wake up, before going out to your business. Pick a mirror, look straight at yourself and say, "Good morning to you." Say it as many times as you can. You can repeat it later in the day as an afternoon dose, as long as it cools you down and makes you live at peace with yourself and all men.

DAVID

King David was an example of a man with a tender heart of forgiveness. As soon as the women of Israel sang his praise louder than that of Saul after his defeat of Goliath, the latter's jealousy was aroused and he sought to kill David night and day. In all his attempts God was with David and would not give him to Saul to kill. On the other hand, David had opportunities to kill his master but he never did. He forgave him all the way through because he considered him as the Lord's anointed. He had an occasion to cut his skirt to prove to him that he could have killed him if he had wanted to but just wouldn't. A lot of us may not be as discerning as that; we would gladly kill and testify in church on Sunday how God gave us the head of our enemy on a platter of gold.

David had every reason to kill his master. Now consider all these: He knew that God had rejected Saul. He knew that, by the will of God, he had been anointed as heir to the throne after Saul's death. Moreover, he knew that the Mosaic Law is an eye for an eye. What else? In all these areas he allowed God to work out his enthronement for him in His own way and timing. Even after Saul's death, David did not take revenge against the household of Saul but went ahead to bless them. What a heart! Are you surprised that he was picked out from the bush and made king by God instead of the more visible brothers who had all kinds of military training?

SOLOMON

God chose Solomon to be king over Israel, after the death of David, because He knew his heart. He was the last person anyone would have considered for that lofty

> Put wisdom as a top priority, because it is through it that kings reign and princes decree justice.

office if we are to judge by the circumstances that brought David and Beersheba together. But God saw beyond what everybody could have considered. He saw in Solomon a tender heart of forgiveness and a passion for people's welfare - the same factors that influenced the choice of David, his father. After Solomon offered a record-breaking sacrifice to God, he was visited in his sleep that same night by God to ask him what He could do for Solomon. Solomon's sacrifice that went up to heaven as a sweet-smelling savour was irresistible and well pleasing to God. If such a blank cheque had been extended to a present-age believer, he would have quoted Luke 6:38, Gal. 6:7 and Mark 10:29-31 to claim back a hundredfold all the animals that had been slain and burnt for the sacrifice. But the main thing Solomon asked for was an understanding heart to rule Israel well. He was totally consumed with the welfare of the people he had been chosen to rule. He also remembered that David his father had instructed him to put wisdom as a top priority, because it is through it that kings reign and princes decree justice (Proverbs 4:1-7; 8:15-16). This pleased God so much that He went ahead to bless him in all things, even beyond what Solomon himself could ever have thought of.

One other striking thing that also moved God was that Solomon never asked for the lives of his enemies. If the Almighty could acknowledge the fact that Solomon had enemies, then he truly had enemies. If it were not an issue, God would not have had to mention it. God knew that it was a common thing for a natural man to desire the death or downfall of his enemies, but Solomon passed the test.

> If the Almighty could acknowledge the fact that Solomon had enemies, then he truly had enemies.

This should serve as a lesson to those who "roast" their neighbours with the fire of the Holy Ghost, as has been made a habit in some churches today. Your true enemies that God wants you to deal with are the devil and his demons, not that "terrible" neighbour of yours next door.

> Your true enemies that God wants you to deal with are the devil and his demons, not that "terrible" neighbour of yours next door.

Solomon's deepest desire was seen in the request he made to God - a heart to rule the people well. The battle belongs to God in the challenges of life. If our access to peace were dependent on how many prayers we make against our enemies, our lives would be very miserable. The good Lord, who neither sleeps nor slumbers, is not wide awake in vain. He is awake to see to our wellbeing, to see us protected and preserved. So stop fretting: your welfare is God's responsibility if you can allow Him to be Lord over your life. This, of course, does not mean that you should be careless with your life; it is only a call that you trust Him more with the issues of your life. Do the little you can and leave the rest for Him to finish.

ABSALOM

The reverse was found in Absalom, whom everybody thought should be king because he was David's first born and the choicest heir to the throne of Israel. He was not in God's good books to rule over His people, despite the fact that he had the heart of all Israel behind him by deception and cunning craftiness (2 Samuel 15:1-6). He was facially handsome but inwardly a wild wolf. God does not see as men see. While men consider, above all things, the externalities, God is more interested in the heart, from where the issues of life spring (Proverbs 4:23). Absalom finally led a rebellion against his father because he wanted to be king by all means; this ultimately led to his death. This should serve as a warning to all bachelors and spinsters who are seeking God's face in marriage. The facial beauty of a woman and the favour you receive from men are all vain and deceptive. The degree to which the fear of God is manifested in a person's life should be your yardstick. Marry "character" - the real person - and not the "building" – his or her body.

Absalom was a wicked schemer with an unforgiving spirit. He killed his half-brother Amnon, after two full years of harbouring bitterness against him for the rape of his sister Tamar. He deceived all of Israel into thinking that he loved them and that he would behave justly when made king, a deceit well known to God. He plotted to overthrow and kill David, his father, who would not die because of God's blessing of long life over him. Can you imagine such a one being favoured to be king? No wonder he lost out.

JOSEPH

Joseph had a tender heart of forgiveness too. Imagine all that his brothers caused him to go through in life. He lost his father's love to a culture and people he never knew. His coat of many colours was reduced to a prison uniform of one colour, on account of an offence he knew nothing about. When you study the Bible very well, you will see that the brothers agreed that he be sold out to Egypt in the anguish of his soul. It was a big trauma for him. Just try to imagine the thoughts that ran through his mind when some unknown men were sending him to an unknown destination, thereby making his expected glorious future thin out into blackness. In spite of all these things, he still chose to forgive. Listen to the confessions of his brothers when he was questioning them in Egypt after God had lifted him up. Can you imagine someone confessing to you how he had severely dealt with you?

> *Genesis 42:21*
> *And they said one to another, we are verily guilty concerning our brother, in that we saw the anguish of his soul, when he besought us, and we would not hear; therefore is this distress come upon us.*

They saw the anguish of his soul when he besought them with tears, but would just not listen because their mercy had been suppressed by the cruelty of envy.

The height of the forgiveness shown to his brothers was seen when Jacob died and his brothers called a high-powered meeting with Joseph in order to stave off revenge. They thought that he soft-pedalled on their judgement because of the presence of their father, whom Joseph loved and respected greatly. Even then, he forgave them. All he said to them was that they meant their attack on him to be evil, but God turned it around for good (Genesis 50:20). Isn't the fact that the ten brothers could conspire against his dream enough to disqualify any one of them? Their decision to harm him was ungodly, and we know that the man is blessed who walks not in the counsel of the ungodly (Psalms 1). That means that you can't be blessed or favoured if you walk in that kind of counsel. How much do you celebrate the achievements of others?

God does not do anything without a reason. His thoughts are very deep. Do you know that He knows the thoughts going on in your mind right now? Some people have not yet been able to buy their dream car despite days

> Good things don't just happen; there are several factors that influence their occurrence.

of protracted fasts, because they have decided never to give a lift to certain people because they did not contribute a dime to their education. This is common in Africa. They save so much but the money to buy the dream car just does not materialise. Some are still attending night vigil after night vigil to get a promotion that just does not come. Why? It is because of what they intend to do with their new "exalted position". Some have filled their hearts with the number of women they will sexually harass, dangling promotion opportunities before them as baits. For others it is a position from which they can inflate contract figures. As long as you refuse to renew your mind to follow God's ways, you will remain stagnated. Good things don't just happen; there are several factors that influence their occurrence.

CHAPTER FIVE

Always Speak The Right Words

Your tongue can either get you favoured or fired. Two forces attend to every word you speak: the positive supernatural and the negative supernatural. Angels attend to right or positive words, while wrong, negative or destructive words attract demon spirits. When I say your tongue, I do not mean the pinkish muscular organ housed in that small enclosure about half an inch below your nose called your mouth. What I am talking about is the effects you create by way of the words you produce.

> Your tongue can either get you favoured or fired.

The deposits you have in your heart are what influence the effects that the tongue produces. In other words, what you have in abundance in your heart is what your tongue rolls out most often. To control your tongue, you must control what you feed into your heart. You must control what books you read, what news you listen to either on radio or on television, what you hear from friends and what kind of pictures you see.

Matthew 12:34b
... For out of the abundance of the heart the mouth speaketh.

The Holy Spirit asked me one day on my way home from a powerful seminar, "Why do you think men speak so negatively rather than positively?" I replied reverently that I didn't know why. He went on and gave me the reason. He said to me that men speak negatively because that is the only thing that attracts their fellow men to help them. They have to sound pitiable and needy. Men only respond to the language of desperation and hopelessness. That is, you cannot be positive and expect help to come to you from men; instead, hatred is what you would get. This is because the ways of God are different from the ways of men.

Psalms 34:2
My soul shall make her boast in the LORD: the humble shall hear thereof, and be glad.

How many men are humble today? Everybody wants to take the glory for their rise in life, even in the ministry. So when you don't talk like a needy person many people get angry, especially the very affluent ones. It is quite understandable why the world is so negative today. You speak the language of the one whose help you need. Since they don't really know God and His saving grace, how can they speak His kind of language? When you speak hopelessly you attract men's sympathy, but remember that vain is the help of any man no matter how highly placed he is (Psalm 118:8).

> You speak the language of the one whose help you need.

It is just like going for social welfare support in Britain and declaring to the authorities concerned that you are rich because Christ became poor for you to be rich. You would never receive any help because your condition must first be very pitiable before they will listen to you. This is why so many people who go for support tell lies in order to paint a very terrible picture of their situation and move the government to act fast. As children of God, we are not pitiable but enviable. We shouldn't talk like defeated people.

You must know that just like words of pity move men to act, so words of power and faith move God to bless us. The government of heaven moves very fast if we can declare victory in the face of apparent defeat, strength when as we are as weak as vegetables, and financial prosperity when there is no dime in our pocket. This is what moves God to act. In God's kingdom we walk by faith, not by sight, because we know that everything is subject to change no matter how deplorable it is. Faith pleases God (Hebrews 11:6), and when God is pleased you can imagine what He will do for you.

The help of man is limited and will not endure for ever. It is only what God does that endures and goes beyond limits. For instance, you can't attempt to own a car or buy a house when on the dole in Britain. In the first place, you will not be able to because the amount you receive is so meagre; secondly, the government will withdraw its support if it becomes aware that you are cruising around with the help it is no longer convinced you need. It is not a social surplus but social support. True help comes from above, and it is above all other help you can ever get. People help you sometimes only to insult you later on account of it. But that is not in the character of God; when God gives gifts He does not take them back. He will never taunt you because of His help, but your uncle's children will know sooner or later that their father contributed to your rise in life, because he may make a reference to it one day when he believes that you are getting too independent.

Romans 11:29
For the gifts and calling of God are without repentance.

I was led to raise an offering for a missionary I met in an assembly at which I was scheduled to preach. It was very unlike me, but I had to respond to the leading of the Holy Spirit. I heard Him clearly. After the offerings were raised and handed over to the missionary, he held the money and began to weep. He demanded that he be allowed to comment in spite of the time constraints we had at that meeting. I bowed to his wish. He said that I had indeed heard from God, because he had declared a few days before that he would never look to any man again in life and that if God would not supply for his missionary work, he would quit the ministry and find something else to do. He went ahead to tell us what informed that decision. There was a man whom God had been using to support him greatly in his mission work.

This man did it with dedication until he got married. One day he went to see the man but, unfortunately, met the new wife, who told the last bit of her mind concerning the financial support the husband had been rendering. The missionary told us that he didn't know how he walked out of the house that day with a vow never again to return for any help whatsoever. He wept uncontrollably and almost cursed the day the Lord made the decision to call him into full-time missionary work. The whole assembly was moved by the pathetic story. I believe that God probably had allowed that to happen so that the missionary's dependence on man would be crushed once and for all. Listen to his declaration again, "If God will not sponsor His work, I'll quit." The very next opportunity God had, He proved Himself mighty on the man's behalf. Keep declaring faith in God. Men will hate you, but the help of God will never be denied you.

POSSESSING THE LAND OF CANAAN

Use your tongue to provoke your deliverance. Moses, the servant of God, sent out twelve spies to spy out the land of Canaan that God had promised them. Ten of them, on their return, brought negative reports of fear that they could not overcome the inhabitants of the land God had given His word about. Their negative report influenced the whole camp, because a majority of the people joined them to confess their inability to reach the Promised Land. All those who had confessed negatively fell out of favour with God. Everyone above the age of twenty who had seen the great acts of God at the parting of the Red Sea and his miracles throughout the journey were to die in the wilderness, just as they had feared. Their words determined their end.

I hate to hear impossibilities; I hate it when people attempt to create fear in me because I know very well that a man is shielded from evil as long as he is fearless. Fear is a great weapon that the devil uses to gain access to people's lives, but faith keeps you out of his reach. Avoid declaring destructive words to yourself. They will not help you one bit. Only Joshua and Caleb who confessed that they were able, by the grace of God, scaled through to the Promised Land.

> Fear is a great weapon that the devil uses to gain access to people's lives, but faith keeps you out of his reach.

ELISHA AND THE KING'S RIGHT-HAND MAN

> There is nothing that provokes your faith or fear as much as the kind of words you speak.

There is nothing that provokes your faith or fear as much as the kind of words you speak. I mean the kind you usually speak, not the kind you spoke just after you attended Brother Kenneth Copeland's or Charles Capps' meeting but the kind you have adopted as a lifestyle even years after the meeting. Elisha once prophesied that within twenty-four hours Israel would be bailed out of a severe famine situation that could be called a national tragedy. The Syrians had besieged Israel and had made life unbearable for them. That had led to their present predicament.

The king's right-hand man felt that the severity of the famine was beyond a day's remedy, despite the mention of God's name in the prophecy. He said that it wasn't possible even if God opened the windows of heaven. He fell out of favour with God. The prophet had some back-up words, a prophecy to seal his fate: "You will only see with your eyes, but you will not taste of it." Despite being healthy and strong, his words handed him over to the torture of death; but not until after he had been promoted to oversee the distribution of what he had said was not possible. The man had no shame at all, because less than twenty-four hours later, he had forgotten what he had said. If I were he, I would have faced the wall like Hezekiah did and would have wept thoroughly before the Lord to reverse the curse before taking over as "distribution manager". It was not an irreversible thing with the force of prayer, because Hezekiah was able to reverse the pronouncement of death on him from God by the Prophet Isaiah. The man fell out of favour with God because he despised Him openly - before all the people who were present when Elisha made that prophecy. Do you think he was the only one who had doubts concerning the dramatic turnaround that had been declared? But because others kept their mouths shut, they were spared.

> *Lamentation 3:37*
> *Who is he that saith, and it cometh to pass, when the Lord commandeth it not?*

ZACHARIAH BECAME DUMB

Zachariah became dumb because he doubted God, in spite of the fact that He sent His archangel to inform him of his deliverance from a long-running barrenness. Zachariah considered his age and that of his wife Elizabeth and felt that he needed a sign from above that could convince him that very old people like them could still bear children. He had forgotten the story of Abraham and Sarah. He was made dumb until John was born. That was the sign the angel Gabriel gave to him.

God knew you would have uncles who were senators, classmates who ended up as governors of states, your town's man who would be so powerful in government. He never connected the source of your livelihood to any of them. He simply said that if you love to live, speak words that are full of life to yourself daily. He knew that there would be terrorists, ritual killers, sicknesses and diseases capable of killing, but He attributed death to the effects that your tongue creates. Your negative word is the key that unlocks the negative situations in your life. We definitely cannot deny the existence of negative situations, but as long as you lock up yourself in the grace of God you are free.

Chapter Five: Always Speak The Right Words

Never give any room to the devil through the looseness of your tongue and the declaration of your fears. Starve him by not giving him any tools to work with. Make him and his demon spirits as redundant as possible by speaking only good words to yourself. Do you know why the devil goes about looking for people to destroy? It is because he cannot kill everybody. Your bad words, not your positive words, are what allow him to find you so easily. The devil will always try to create fear in people. He sells you the idea of being careful to speak positive words just so that you don't lose face and become the butt of people's jokes if the reverse happens. The truth is that those words prove to be great barriers to him. It is just like people telling you not to allow the seed of corn you want to plant to be seen by anybody so that when it begins to germinate it does not turn into yam. Does that make any sense? Don't ever forget that what the devil fears most in your life is what he intimidates you with most.

> Never give any room to the devil through the looseness of your tongue and the declaration of your fears. Starve him by not giving him any tools to work with.

The cheapest way to handle your enemies is by knowing how to control your tongue. The wages of sin is death. So if you don't commit any blunder with your mouth, you can be very sure that you are safe. A kept tongue is a kept life. If you can tame your tongue, you do not need to go to a school of theology for a Bachelor's in demonology. With the understanding of how words operate, you already have a Master's and a PhD. Whatever makes you master the devil is a Master's degree as far as I am concerned. And whatever makes you establish your dominion or power over the host of the devil is a PhD. Isn't it?

Psalm 39:1
I said, I will take heed to my ways, that I sin not with my tongue: I will keep my mouth with a bridle, while the wicked is before me.

> Don't ever forget that what the devil fears most in your life is what he intimidates you with most.

The devil and his demons are the wicked in question. Do not forget that these spirits are everywhere and they are out to do more wickedness in these last days. Since you know you carry in you what can either kill you or make you live, it is highly advisable that you guard it very well. Esau probably did not know the eternal effects that words could create. He swore at will on Jacob's demand that he (Jacob) was the elder. He looked around and thought that since no one could stand as a witness for Jacob that he ever swore such an oath, he swore at will and went on his way with the "takeaway" pottage. He probably felt that what he said was limited to that day and that region. He possibly thought that there were no witnesses to his birth. He never knew that words are powerful enough to influence destiny, both positively or negatively. Heaven recorded it and declared Jacob as the first born from then on. God did that because whatever you utter is what He is committed to do unto you.

> *Exodus 4:22-23 (Emphasis mine)*
> *And thou shalt say unto Pharaoh, Thus saith the LORD, Israel (Jacob) is my son even <u>my firstborn</u>: And I say unto thee, let my son go, that he may serve me: and if thou refuse to let him go, behold, I will slay thy son, even <u>thy firstborn</u>.*

I say this by revelation that I couldn't care less about what circumstances have surrounded your birth, your words can change things. Jacob came out second but the

> I say this by revelation that I couldn't care less about what circumstances have surrounded your birth, your words can change things.

words of Esau caused the spiritual exchange and he became the first born, with the rights to all the benefits thereof. Likewise, no matter how wonderful your redemptive rights are in Christ, if you speak what Satan wants you to say, God will not bail you out because He never bailed Esau out even though he was a seed of Abraham. That means that as He hears you confess favour night and day, He will surely visit you because He is faithful to every one of His good promises (1Kings 8:56b). As you keep declaring His word concerning your life, the Spirit of God is committed to stirring the hearts of people to bring those words to pass. The angels of God are also committed to make good His word. They listen attentively to carry out every instruction we give in the will of God and in the name of Jesus Christ of Nazareth. God raised up Cyrus, a heathen king, to make provisions for the rebuilding of the destroyed temple at Jerusalem just in order to cause His words, by the mouth of Jeremiah his prophet, to come to pass.

Ezra 1:1-2

Now in the first year of Cyrus king of Persia, that the word of the LORD by the mouth of Jeremiah might be fulfilled, the LORD stirred up the spirit of Cyrus king of Persia, that he made a proclamation throughout all his kingdom, and put it also in writing, saying, Thus saith Cyrus king of Persia. The LORD God of heaven hath given me all the kingdoms of the earth; and he hath charged me to build him an house at Jerusalem, which is in Judah.

God can stir up anybody to help you too. Stop looking to your uncle or your affluent friends. Cyrus was not a Jew, but in order that God's word should be fulfilled by all means, He stirred him up to do what someone had declared years back. The fact that some of the words you have declared earlier have not materialised does not mean that they will not. In consistency lies the power of faith confessions. The man Cyrus probably didn't know what he was doing because he was under an influence greater than him. Mind you, it was God's word but by the mouth of Jeremiah. You too can declare God's word with your mouth to cause God to move people of calibre on your behalf.

In the new covenant, you have a better covenant than the one in which Jeremiah operated. If the Holy Ghost could move on his behalf, He will move much more on your behalf today. You have a surer word of prophecy in the written word of God. Open it and read all His good promises. They will never be found wanting in every issue of life that you send them to attack. Your own Cyrus will be stirred up to make provisions for your ministry, your marriage, and your education in Jesus' mighty name.

I have discovered some important areas where the body of Christ has been getting it wrong in this issue of positive confession. First, we are grossly uninformed about the good promises of God and that they are capable of making us live a heavenly life here on earth.

2 Peter 1:4
Whereby are given unto us exceeding great and precious promises: that by these ye might be partakers of the divine nature, having escaped the corruption that is in the world through lust.

Messages of faith are highly criticised in some quarters; as if without faith it is possible for anyone to please God. On the other hand, we hardly believe what we read on the pages of our Bibles. We see them as mere stories, not too different from the news we read in our daily paper. The Bible is an inspiration from God by His Spirit. We need the same Holy Spirit to open us to the truth in it. Prosperity is in there, yet many are poor. Mighty children are there, yet barren cases are very prevalent. We have marital bliss, yet divorce cases seem an impossible task for even the church to handle. Only the Holy Spirit can open our eyes to the truth assigned to quench our thirst in every wilderness in which we find ourselves.

> Only the Holy Spirit can open our eyes to the truth assigned to quench our thirst in every wilderness in which we find ourselves.

Hagar wept together with Ishmael in their quest for water in their wilderness of thirst. It was not until a divine hand touched her eyes that she could see the well of water nearby, which quenched her thirst. Weeping is not the answer; it is the search for the light in the Word that can cause us to rise and shine. That light will never shine until the Word gains entrance into our spirits. The mere fact that you doubt that your confessions will come to pass destroys the power to make them productive. Like a man of God once said, "God will never say no to your demands if your faith says yes."

Hebrews 11: 6
But without faith it is impossible to please him: for he that comes to God must believe that he is, and that he is a rewarder of them that diligently seek him.

One more thing is that Christians want to say something today and have it the very next day. Patience is needed in everything we do in life. Your faith, too, needs patience if it is to produce. To be patient does not mean to be idle, doing nothing, or to say something once and keep quiet, waiting for a manifestation that may never come. To be patient is to be constant, to maintain your confession and attitude the same way all the time, regardless of whether you can see an immediate physical proof or not. Since that confession and attitude are what you believe, you must continue in them. You will provoke favour everywhere and every time when all these points are heeded.

> To be patient is to be constant, to maintain your confession and attitude the same way all the time, regardless of whether you can see an immediate physical proof or not.

CHAPTER SIX

Live Expecting To Be Shown Favour

Proverbs 23:18
For surely there is an end; and thine expectation shall not be cut off.

We are the city put upon the hill that cannot be hidden - Matthew 5:14. We are the ones that God has blessed above all the peoples or nations of the earth - Deuteronomy 7:14. We are the royal and peculiar people that God has called out of darkness to reflect His glorious light on earth - 1 Peter 2:9. We are the ones that God said He would use other people's lives to save ours if need be - Isaiah 43:4. We are the ones who are to lend to nations and borrow from no one - Deuteronomy 28:12. We are the ones that the Lord has declared He would never leave nor forsake - Hebrews 13:5. We are the anointed of the Lord that God has commanded never to be harmed nor hurt in any way - Psalm 105:14-15. We

> We are not called to be ruined but to reign in majesty and honour.

are the ones He has made priests and kings unto God to reign on the planet earth - Revelation 1:6 & 5:10. We are not called to be ruined but to reign in majesty and honour. We are the ones God calls the apple of His precious eye - Zechariah 2:8. We are the ones He calls His beloved and cherished ones, but how come the reverse is the case with most of us Christians? How come we live expecting more evil things to happen to us than good? Should we even expect anything evil since we know that our expectations will never be cut off?

We live expecting to be rejected and put down at work or at school. We live expecting to be marginalised and humiliated one way or the other by society at large. We expect all these in the name of persecution, but we are wrong. The fact that Jesus said we would be persecuted is not a licence to accept defeat and expect the worst in life. Jesus said that though persecution will come one way or the other because of the devil who hates to see us as God's children, we are to be of good cheer because He has defeated the evil one for us. We face only one side of that scripture - the persecution - and leave out the second part

- the eternally established defeat of Satan and his hosts.

We must live expecting that something good will happen to us one way or the other. Wake up in the morning expecting that some one will do you good as you step out of your house to go about your business. What you don't expect you don't experience. This is a fact of life that we must not ignore in any way. When you wake up in the morning, declare that it is the day the Lord God has made in which you will rejoice and be glad. Declare that since God daily loads us with benefits, He will use someone to deliver your own parcel of benefits for the day. I know that the benefits spoken about may not always be in terms of materialism, but at least expect someone to show you some kindness. This expectation will break the hold of racism or rejection that anyone may attempt to mete out against you. Haven't you seen someone helping you and telling you that he doesn't know why he's doing that?

A man once helped me and told me that he knew he was under some kind of spell that he couldn't resist. He thought that I had used some kind of voodoo on him. I had prayed with a group of people and went to him expecting something good from him, which he couldn't deny me. So when travelling to a nation to which you haven't been before, expect God to position people there who are waiting to do you good. Just expect it and before you know it you will begin to enjoy the kind of favour that you have never experienced before in life. I taught about this in one of my meetings and the very next day someone called to testify. He was in a queue at the airport when an official from the airline he was travelling with came up to him and instructed that he should be upgraded to a first-class seat that he did not pay for. What about that?

Do not expect that someone will gun you down. Do not expect that someone will be racist against you. Do not expect that you will lose out on that job interview you're preparing for. Do not expect that you will be refused that visa you are applying for. Do not expect that your children will be abused when you are not around to keep watch over them. Do not expect that you will be given a high interest rate on your mortgage, expect favour to give you the best rate. Always expect that for you there will be an exception for good and not evil.

I got a very sad letter closing the savings account I had opened when I first came to England, with a warning from the bank that it would never have anything further to do with me now and in the future, for a mistake I counted as very minimal. I had made the mistake of putting my employer's address as my residence address, and that was it. It was not the closure of the account that was painful but the tone of the letter, which made it seem as though I was the greatest fraudster of all time. Against all advice, I took the letter and went to see the branch manager, expecting that the favour of God was going to do the magic. It did. He apologised for the tone used and right there opened another account for me, this time a current account. "By the way, you would be limited in your dealings with a savings account," he said.

Job said that what he had feared, in other words what he had expected, had happened to him. Job expected that things would not be rosy all the time and that some day he would lose all that he had, and that was exactly what he experienced.

Job 3:25
For the thing which I greatly feared is come upon me, and that which I was afraid is come unto me.

Clemence Westerhorf, one-time coach of the Nigerian football team the Super Eagles, amazed me in an interview I watched in late 1993 as he prepared to jet out to Algiers for the last game to qualify for the USA 1994 World Cup. He kept declaring that he would take Nigeria to its first World Cup ever. When asked what he would do if he failed in his bid to take Nigeria there, he replied he had not prepared and would not prepare any speech or action for failure, because he was going to succeed. Everything the interviewer did to make him say what he would do if he didn't succeed fell on the deaf ears of a man whose heart was as hard as a brick wall in his resolve that he would succeed. I mean, this was a man who was facing an away match with Algeria. He got a draw with barely three minutes to full time and gave Nigeria the World Cup ticket. He never expected to lose and he didn't lose. He worked hard at it and got his desired expectation.

Reggae singer Peter Tosh sang that he was wanted dead or alive by evil forces and that there was no hiding place for him. He was ultimately shot dead by some assailants on September 11, 1987. Elvis Presley was always quoted as saying that he would die at the same age as his mother because of their connection in spirit, soul and body. He died at years; the same age as his mother Gladys' official age, since it was believed that she reduced her age by 4 years to appear younger.

The woman with the issue of blood in Mark's gospel chapter 5 expected that she would be healed as soon as she touched the hem of Jesus' garment and that was exactly what she experienced. The fountain of her blood dried up immediately.

The lame man at the gate called beautiful looked at Peter and John, expecting to receive something from them. He expected something and got more than money. He got back his legs and leaped for joy.

> *Acts 3:5 (additions mine)*
> *And he (the lame man) gave heed unto them (Peter and John), expecting to receive something from them.*

These are my conclusions: Any man filled with fear will expect evil, while one filled with faith will expect good, both of which cannot but take place sooner or later. The second thing to take good note of is that you must work at your expectations. If

> **Any man filled with fear will expect evil, while one filled with faith will expect good, both of which cannot but take place sooner or later.**

> Lack of good expectations will mar any man's chances of becoming successful in life.

you expect to pass your exams, then let that expectation push you to read well for them. Lack of good expectations will mar any man's chances of becoming successful in life.

CHAPTER SEVEN

The Beauty Of Humility

The devil is the author of pride. He was once an angel of God named Lucifer, the bright and morning star. He was made from every precious stone created by God and could be described as having a perfect finish. He was called beautiful, even though we know that angels have the masculine gender from a Biblical perspective.

Lucifer was a creature who could be described as made for purpose. He led the worship of God with absolute ease and dexterity. Every musical instrument he ever needed to lead the worship of God effectively was built into him. All the musical pipe works were perfectly arranged in him. This made his job an effortless one. He never needed to strike a guitar string, beat a drum or carry a saxophone to blow. When he led worship, all the musical arrangements for each worship session were the products of his thoughts. He expressed the worship of God effortlessly, just the way a man without a breathing problem breathes out through his nostrils.

No other angel or archangel of God could be compared to him in beauty. He stood taller than every other angel in beauty and in his musical prowess. He was the envy of all other angels; no wonder he commanded so much respect from them that he was to able to win about a third over to his side in his plot to overthrow the Most High God (Revelation 12:4). He was a perfect and loyal creature until the iniquity of pride was found in him.

The devil still tries to sow the seed of pride into people today. He does this to cause us to fall out of favour with God. He knows very well that God resists the proud and gives grace to the humble. Our duty is to say "no" to all his schemes and to let God be given the glory for every accomplishment we enjoy today. The cure for pride is innate in every man; just refuse to usurp God's glory when men try to pass it on to you. Always remember that without God, you cannot achieve anything meaningful in life. Like one man of God rightly put it, "I am not an achiever but a receiver, because there is nothing we have that we didn't receive in the first place."

Chapter Seven: The Beauty Of Humility

Pride plagues people and, of course, nothing demotes like pride. It is very subtle because it tries to disguise itself as much as possible so that its victims do not go free unless they are punished. A man of God described pride like this: It is like a man inflating a balloon and not knowing when to stop. What happens? The balloon gets blown up and torn into pieces. Now listen to the consequences: The balloon is lost, and even if you attempt to regain it, it can never be as whole as it was before. The air in the balloon is gone, and you will never get the volume of air you intended the balloon to contain even if you attempt to inflate the torn balloon after tying the shredded parts together. The purpose of inflating the balloon in the first place is lost.

Another person described pride as the letter "I" in the middle of the word pride itself, always attempting to stand taller than the remaining four letters PRDE. In other words, don't let the self in you rise above others. Always prefer others to yourself, because this was Paul's admonition in one of the epistles.

Romans 12:10
Be kindly affectioned one to another with brotherly love; in honour preferring one another.

> We will sin less if we are not self-seeking.

What you have to know about pride is that it shares the same letter "I" with the word sin. We can conclude that they both have the same root cause, self-promotion or self-priority. We will sin less if we are not self-seeking. We will be humble if we are not out to project ourselves as being better than others. One thing we have to know about pride, which most of its victims have not sat down to analyse, is that it often does not help us achieve what we employ it for. We want to be more accepted, but it turns out to be the reason most people are turned off.

> One thing we have to know about pride, which most of its victims have not sat down to analyse, is that it often does not help us achieve what we employ it for.

Pride has sunk the high and the low, the rich and the poor, the educated and the uneducated, the beautiful and the ugly, male and female and so on. It has no respect for anybody. It has caused countless numbers of people to fall out of favour with God and with man. It plagued Uzziah, making him think that he could do the work of a priest to which God did not call him, but simply because he was a king he usurped the priest's authority, to his own shame. He became leprous afterwards and never recovered from the disease until his death. Pride turned Nebuchadnezzar into a beast and he ate grass for seven years until mercy found him again. Pride sank Pharaoh and his hosts at the Red Sea and did not spare the head of Goliath. Pride has no regard for whatever God does because it has itself to give the glory to. The only cure for it is humility and until it is cured it brings to a halt the flow of God's favour.

I learnt something from the statement of evangelist Reinhard Bonnke while preaching in one of his worldwide crusades. He said, "If the Bible is too old, read your newspapers because you can learn the same lessons from them." I quite agree with him in the context in which he made the statement. If we don't believe Biblical prophecies, at least we can read about world events and know that something significant is about to happen that will bring the whole world to a standstill. This is the imminent coming of our great King and Lord. I was in the Westminster area of London recently and I saw a poster that caught my attention. It

> If the Bible is too old, read your newspapers.

read, "Jesus the greatest comeback." These are some of the things you may come across in the street that will preach the same thing to you.

> Nothing destroys a glorious destiny like pride.

Nothing destroys a glorious destiny like pride. It is a silent killer that has paralysed so many people while remaining undetected. In agreement with Evangelist Bonnke, I watched an interview granted to one of Nigeria's overly gifted footballers. At the time of the interview he was still fully in form and never could imagine that everything we are, here on earth, we are by the special grace of our great God. One could see pride glaringly all over him in his attempts to answer the questions he was asked. To end the interview, this was his closing remark, either out of sheer arrogance or mistake: "Without me, no Eagles." (The Super Eagles is the name of the Nigerian national team.) If the Bible is too old to teach us that pride destroys, I was able to see from that interview that pride sinks destinies, because that was about the last time the footballer in question kicked a ball for his nation. It was like an incurable injury was waiting for him to finish his interview before striking. And indeed, no sooner had he made that statement than he got injured and had to quit active football. To make that statement in a country of about one hundred and fifty million people was daring.

"One can never go wrong being humble." I heard this wise saying from a friend when we were sharing the Word one day. Before I was born again, I used to have a friend who wouldn't accept that humility pays. We often confuse self-esteem with pride. They are different. Self-esteem is the correct estimation of who you are. This helps you overcome an inferiority complex among your peers. Pride, on the other hand, is an overestimation of oneself and is wrong. This friend of mine, in my humble opinion, was full of himself. He learnt the lesson of his life when we went on a business appointment to see the MD of a company about a proposal he had made. It was actually his appointment, but because we had other places to go after the meeting, I went with him to the office in question. On arrival, he bypassed the pretty receptionist and went straight to the MD's office. He beckoned to me to come along, but I wouldn't. I knew that his actions could cause embarrassment. My guess was right, because after about

> "One can never go wrong being humble."

a minute or so, he came out to see the receptionist to fill out a form. The expression on his face was sullen. I knew that was not the right place to start my enquiry. He probably had wanted to "pose" for the pretty girl. On our way back, however, I summoned the courage to ask what had happened to make him come back and fill out the form. "The silly man sent me out, saying that the secretary was not there as a decoration," he blurted out. Once again, the whole message had been preached: if the Bible is too old, read your newspapers or check events around you.

An interesting thing happened to me one morning after I had finished a night shift and was on my way home. That was when I still had a secular job as a boiler engineer. One of our staff who had been under my supervision in another department met me at the gate, as he was about to clock in for his morning duty. "Your worship Sir," he said. I replied sharply that I thought God alone should be worshipped. He didn't quite see what I was trying to let him know. Or better put, he didn't want to appreciate the point I was trying to make. This got me mad at him. I could see a bit of sycophancy on display. "Never greet me again in that manner if you don't know how to say a simple good morning," I said in anger. The madder I got, the more he downplayed the whole issue and the more I embarrassed myself with my shouts. The looks on the faces of all those around revealed the thoughts of their hearts: a "spiritual" brother has blown a fuse because of the way I had raised my voice in anger to refute the early morning satanic greeting. So I went near a small tree in front of the gate and asked quietly, "Holy Spirit, are you angry with me because of the anger I displayed before everyone?" I heard an emphatic "no" inside me. I thought it was my mind justifying me, so I asked the same question again. The second time I heard the same thing, "no". I pleaded with the Holy Spirit, but this time around I asked Him to kindly give me a scriptural reference to justify my nasty actions. "Those who praised Herod didn't die with him," He said. This to me meant that I was only saving my life by my actions.

To understand His answer better, I will briefly let you know what happened to Herod. He sat upon his throne one day to address his people and because of his oratory power, or out of sheer sycophancy, his admirers concluded that his voice was no longer that of a man but God's. He was very pleased with his listeners for equating him with the Almighty rather than fighting back to give all the glory to God. An angel of God struck him right there on his seat of power. From nowhere, mysterious worms came over him and ate him to death. All this happened because he usurped the glory meant for God.

Acts 12:21-23
And upon a set day Herod, arrayed in royal apparel, sat upon his throne, and made an oration unto them. And the people gave a shout, saying, it is the voice of a god, and not a man. And immediately the angel of the Lord smote him, because he gave not God the glory: and he was eaten of worms, and gave up the ghost.

Let us remember that no one ever goes wrong being humble. Adherence to this admonition will bring you nothing but favour before God and man. In the words of John Hagee, "The favour of God will disappear at the first appearance of pride."

CHAPTER EIGHT

The Praise Dimension

Nobody ever gets angry when being praised. I have never met anyone who has, except of course if the person knows that he's just being flattered. When a man is praised, he's happy and is most often highly motivated to do better. The reverse is the case when you continually criticise a man. After a while, he'll begin to lose confidence in himself. Rather than improving, his productivity may begin to dwindle. Of course, why should any man kill himself for someone who does not see anything good in him?

Jesus came to His own people with an open heart to save, heal and prosper them immensely, but when they rejected Him, He looked elsewhere with His loving arms wide open to whosoever would receive Him. That is why you and I have the privilege of being saved today.

John 1:11-12
He came unto his own, and his own received him not. But as many as received him, to them gave he power to become the sons of God, even to them that believe in his name.

> **Never go to a place where you are tolerated; go to where you are celebrated.**

Never go to a place where you are tolerated; go to where you are celebrated. It is where you are celebrated that the potential of God in you can be acknowledged and helped to the limelight.

> **When you are angry don't talk and when you are happy avoid making promises.**

I was at a friend's wedding when the officiating minister made a statement that has stayed with me ever since. He said, "When you are angry don't talk and when you are happy avoid making promises, because you may never be able to keep them." How true that is. Consider what happened to King Herod, who gave an order against his own wishes. He ordered that the head of John the Baptist be removed from his neck.

On his birthday, Herod had promised the daughter of Herodias to ask for anything up to half of his kingdom and he would grant it. This gesture was on account of her skilful dance display in the presence of all the invited dignitaries. The innocent girl was influenced by her mother to ask for the head of John the Baptist, the Prophet, who had always kicked against her affairs with the king. Herodias had never liked John the Baptist ever since the Prophet had declared that it was unlawful for Herod to snatch her from his brother Philip. Because of the Baptist's stand against her infidelity, she had always looked for an opportunity to deal with him. The opportunity finally came when Herod was careless with his tongue. Herod made the promise because he was so happy, but he could not undo the innocent girl's request, having sealed it with an oath before his dignitaries.

Matthew 14: 6-11
But when Herod's birthday was kept, the daughter of Herodias danced before them, and pleased Herod. Whereupon he promised with an oath to give her whatsoever she would ask. And she, being before instructed of her mother, said, Give me here John Baptist's head in a charger. And the king was sorry: nevertheless for the oath's sake, and them which sat

with him at meat, he commanded it to be given her. And he sent, and beheaded John in the prison. And his head was brought in a charger, and given to the damsel: and she brought it to her mother.

Herod could not swallow his pride in front of all his guests, but went ahead to kill an innocent Prophet of God. For all he cared, he had thought she would ask for a palatial mansion or request a custom-built chariot. But what she asked for was the head of a poor Prophet that was of no use to her.

Do you know that God Himself has promised that when we praise Him, He will so bless us that all the ends of the earth will be afraid? How many times have we sat down to think that the integrity of God is at stake if He does not live up to our expectations? Now, can we compare the integrity of a wife snatcher to that of the thrice-holy King of the universe?

Psalm 97:12
Rejoice in the LORD, ye righteous; and give thanks at the remembrance of his holiness.

No wonder that the Psalmist gave the advice in the

Bible passage highlighted above by admonishing us always to give thanks to God at the remembrance of His holiness. Why? Because he knew too well that a Holy God such as ours would always keep His promises to His children. Holiness and falsehood can never go together. Do you know that this simple truth is enough to produce faith in anyone who is finding it difficult to trust God? Go ahead and praise God for all His goodness with faith in your heart that the exercise will unlock favour in every area of your life.

> *Psalm 67:3-7*
> *Let the people praise thee, O God; let all the people praise thee. O let the nations be glad and sing for joy: for thou shalt judge the people righteously, and govern the nations upon earth. Selah. Let the people praise thee, O God; let all the people praise thee. Then shall the earth yield her increase; and God, even our own God, shall bless us. God shall bless us; and all the ends of the earth shall fear him.*

The ends of the earth were afraid when Sarah gave birth to Isaac, because medical science is yet to give an explanation for it. The whole world was afraid when Lazarus was raised from the dead after spending four days in the grave, because it destroyed the doctrine of the Sadducees who do not believe in resurrection. It equally dealt a blow to the belief systems of the Pharisees, who reckon that a man is only dead after three days. They believe that his spirit hovers around for the first three days before finally returning to his Maker. In other words, all the people whom Jesus claimed to have raised from the dead before Lazarus were seen as false claims. The whole world was afraid when Meschach, Shedrach and Abednego came out alive from Nebucchadnezzar's fiery furnace, a fire that was hot enough to kill even those who threw them into it. The whole world was afraid when the Red Sea parted and the children of Israel came out of Egypt on dry ground. The whole world was afraid when the walls of Jericho fell down flat after a shout in the praise of God and His glorious power. Above all, the whole world was afraid when Jesus rose from the dead on the third day.

> **The minimum qualification you need to have to praise God is your breath.**

God is still able to do the same and much more today, if you give Him the highest praise He deserves. The minimum qualification you need to have to praise God is your breath.

Psalm 150:6
Let everything that has breath, praise the Lord.

God is not waiting for you to have a car first. He's not waiting for you to build your house first. He's not waiting for everything in your life to be put right first. As long as you have your breath, praise Him! Are you in the hospital? He's not waiting for you to be well first, go ahead and just praise Him with the little strength you have.

Let me make this point very clear so that you can get the best out of the praise of God: praise should be done as an act of obedience to God and never utilised as a channel for collecting goodies from Him. If you do it with the desire to receive blessings, then you will end up more frustrated than ever. I can say with full assurance that God will turn deaf ears to it. Praise Him because He's dependable. Praise Him because He's ever in control of circumstances and situations. Praise Him because His mercies are new

> Praise should be done as an act of obedience to God and never utilised as a channel for collecting goodies from Him.

every morning - that is why you're still alive and well. Praise Him because He's Lord of all! Amen!

> True praise provokes God from His heart to heal, to bless and to deliver whoever does it.

True praise provokes God from His heart to heal, to bless and to deliver whoever does it. Praise also goes beyond dancing and singing merely to "feel" good. It is a heart-to-heart communication with God, appreciating Him in all things (no matter how bad). It can later lead you to dance and jump, but your self will have been brought to it's lowest point before that.

There was a hopeless case of a man who was possessed with a legion of demons, no fewer than two thousand of them. His case was so pathetic that most psychiatric homes rejected him because of the peculiarity of his madness. I would call it a first-class madness. A man of God once joked that when lunatics saw him, they took off, calling him mad. Mental homes that, on compassionate grounds, had attempted to admit him for treatment had themselves to blame later on. Every time chains were used to bind him to enable them to administer the necessary medication, he cut the chains into pieces, causing everybody to run for their lives. He would escape and return to the tombs he was taken away from until everybody left him to his fate. But a day came when he provoked favour to secure his total deliverance by a singular bow to Jesus. He saw Jesus afar off and ran to bow in worship of the King. The demons that once oppressed him knew that they were in trouble because a man cannot serve two masters; you cannot worship Jesus and madness at the same time. It is a spiritual law that a man cannot serve two masters.

Mark 5:2-8
And when he was come out of the ship, immediately there met him out of the tombs a man with an unclean spirit, who had his dwelling among the tombs; and no man could bind him, no, not with chains: because he had been often bound with fetters and chains, and the chains had been plucked asunder by him, and the fetters broken in pieces: neither could any man tame him.

And always, night and day, he was in the mountains, and in the tombs, crying, and cutting himself with stones. But when he saw Jesus afar off, he ran and worshipped him, and cried with a loud voice, and said, what have I to do with thee, Jesus, thou Son of the Most High God? I adjure thee by God, that thou torment me not. For he said unto him, come out of the man, thou unclean spirit.

You can do the same thing today, no matter how far away you are from Jesus. The guilt of past sins may be creating a gulf, but you can bridge it by confessing them and moving on with Jesus. You think that He has forgotten about you and all your labours of love, but a single sincere bow will disprove that. You might have been deceived that your name has been deleted from the Lord's plans and that all those prophecies for your life may never come to pass again. Hear the good news: the Lord is passing your way today through this book. A single bow will disprove Satan's lies totally.

To have this God-ordained anointed book in your hand is not a mistake. If God truly orders the steps of His Saints, then He has ordered this book into your hand. It is enough proof that you will rise again. Believe that you will rise again, that you will be celebrated again. *A man who wanders out of the way of understanding shall remain in the congregation of the dead, Proverbs 21:16.* The mad man wandered from the understanding that he was created for a purpose. He knew nothing about the spiritual verity that weeping may endure for a night but joy comes in the morning. He remained in his situation until the day He was able to thank God - not for his situation, but in his situation. And the whole ugly situation was turned around.

If a mad man of that calibre could have a future with God, how about you? Do you know the prophecies that probably went before him the day he was born, that made the devil so mad that he plagued him to that extent? Heaven and earth may pass away, but not a jot of God's word concerning you will ever go unfulfilled. You are probably going through what you are today because the wicked one is fighting the word about your life. Don't give up. Just go ahead and worship God the more. Praise Him the more. The mad man saw Jesus afar off, but it did not discourage Him. Praise God all the way. You may think that God is far off because you think He's not concerned about you, but go ahead and give Him praise. Praise Him in the morning. Praise Him during your lunch break. Praise Him when driving home from your office. Praise Him on your bed. Praise Him when flying in an aeroplane. God enjoys it.

I left the office late one night, before I bought my car,

and was by the roadside in front of my company waiting for a taxi. I began to tell the Lord how much I loved and appreciated Him. Suddenly, a man who was driving by in his car saw me and tried to apply his brakes about four times, as if in doubt whether or not to stop. Finally, he did stop and reversed to where I was standing and asked if he could give me a lift to where I was going. He said that something inside him said that he should stop and pick me up, but he had to battle a bit within himself, knowing how complex the city of Lagos can be. That is the kind of favour that sincere worship can bring.

I had an excess luggage fee waived on one of my international trips. I thought that the white woman at the counter had made a mistake, but she smiled and said, "Young man, I am conscious of what I am doing." I remember that I worshipped God tremendously that morning. A few minutes after I had told Jesus how much I loved and cherished Him on another occasion, a young man came into the clothes shop where I was and asked me to pick any of the clothes on display that I liked. As if that were not enough, he added a very beautiful umbrella to what I picked. Later, he said that my first book on the power of the tongue had blessed him.

Chapter Eight: The Praise Dimension

After an evening service one Sunday, a parishioner walked up to me and led me to the altar where I had finished preaching. "I want this altar to be a witness between us that I am giving you my car from the depth of my heart." When I asked why he was giving me his car, he replied, "Because I like you." I remember that a period of quality praise had preceded this time. Now in a place like London, it is worthy of thanksgiving and praise. I could go on and on about how much of God's favour I have experienced in the place of praise. Praise works wonders, I must confess.

CHAPTER NINE

The Force Of Loyalty

The devil fell out of favour with God because his initial loyalty was tampered with by pride. This caused some of the angels that fell with him, in his rebellion, to abandon their first place. Everybody talks about how he fell through pride, but very few have sat down to consider that the thing that brought about pride was disloyalty in his heart.

From the fall of man in Eden, loyalty has become a very scarce commodity. This is because inside the forbidden fruit that Adam and Eve ate was the seed of selfishness and self-centredness. The traits were revealed when the Almighty showed up to ask why they had eaten the forbidden fruit. Adam couldn't explain why, so he shifted the blame onto God and the woman He had blessed him with. Eve's tainted soul could not be concealed either - she passed the blame onto the serpent, their former pet.

From the fall of man in Eden, loyalty has become a

very scarce commodity. The immediate effect of partaking of the forbidden fruit was that the pair took on the nature of Satan. What the evil fruit injected into the human race was selfishness and self-centredness. Only having a thoroughly renewed mind in Christ can stop all these. Is

> From the fall of man in Eden, loyalty has become a very scarce commodity.

it not amazing that Absalom could not wait for King David to die before attempting to overthrow him? He schemed his way into the hearts of the people against his own father. But thank goodness, he could not penetrate the heart of God who is the Judge. He openly discredited the judgment passed by his father in a matter between opposing parties, thereby discrediting David's wisdom.

Absalom's end was a shameful death by hanging. He never got to the throne he craved passionately. The issue of loyalty cannot be overridden by a biological or blood relationship. We can see that not even a father-son relationship can thwart its demands.

> The issue of loyalty cannot be overridden by a biological or blood relationship.

Absalom died prematurely because God does not

> No disloyal man or woman has a future in any establishment; the dry land is their lot.

approve of disloyalty. The `only exception to this is if someone above you wants you to walk against God by his actions. A case in point was Peter's revolt against the religious leaders of his day, who would not permit him to use the name of Jesus for his crusades. No disloyal man or woman has a future in any establishment; the dry land is their lot. Have you ever seen a man who has not sold out to an establishment prospering in it? It is a difficult thing, because God's spiritual law forbids it.

> *Psalms 68:6*
> *God setteth the solitary in families: he bringeth out those who are bound with chains: but the rebellious dwell in a dry land.*

Loyalty is a spirit and that is why it is not taught in our secular schools. The Bible speaks of Joshua and Caleb's loyalty to God and Moses. What made them bring back encouraging reports from their espionage was because they had a different spirit. This made them hang on, while the other ten spies backed out and rebelled against

God and Moses because of the sight of the intimidating giants they saw in the land they had spied on.

> *Numbers 14:24*
> *But my servant Caleb, because he had another spirit with him, and had followed me fully, him will I bring into the land where into he went; and his seed shall possess it.*

BENEFICIARIES OF LOYALTY

The lists of those who were favoured because of their loyalty are endless, but we shall look at a few.

RUTH

Ruth probably would have remained a widow all her life after the death of her husband. Had it not been for her loyalty to her dead husband and her faith in the God of the Jews, she would have just been a footnote in history. She was a Moabite woman from a background of paganism, yet she would not let go of her mother-in-law and her God. She took a risk despite not having answers to the spell that was upon the late husband's family. How could a father and his two sons die mysteriously within a short time without any explanations of the cause of their death? It seems that she damned the consequence that stared her in the face – that any woman married to the family would soon taste widowhood. Yet she pressed on.

Let us hear the resolved voice of loyalty as Ruth clung to her mother-in-law Naomi when she was returning to her native land of Israel, having lost her husband and two sons, one of which Ruth married.

Ruth 1:16
And Ruth said, Entreat me not to leave thee, or to return from following after thee: for whither thou goest, I will go; and where thou lodgest, I will lodge: thy people shall be my people and thy God my God.

The outcome of that vow is known today: she got married to one of the wealthiest men in Israel. She became a paternal great-grandmother to King David, Israel's greatest king ever. Moreover, she is in the lineage of the Lord of the universe, Jesus Christ.

ELISHA

This extraordinary Prophet of God was favoured with double the anointing of Elijah his boss on the platform of unreserved loyalty. He never went back despite pleas from his boss to stop following him because he was to be taken up to heaven soon. He kept going from Gilgal to Bethel to Jericho to Jordan, until Elijah had to ask him what he needed from him that made him so resolute in following him all the way. "A double portion of your anointing," Elisha replied. "Consider it done if you see me when I am taken up to heaven," said Elijah. In other words, if you can be faithful to the end, you'll have what you want. Elisha passed the test and soon became both the envy of and master over the other sons of the prophets who were his ex-colleagues.

> *2 Kings 2:15*
> *And when the sons of the prophets which were to view at Jericho saw him, they said, the spirit of Elijah dost rest on Elisha. And they came to meet him, and bowed themselves to the ground before him.*

Loyalty does not reduce people; it will only place you over those who think that you are being foolish or outdated serving a fellow man. Elisha's former colleagues bowed to the ground before him. What a lift!

PETER

A lot of people see Peter as the one who denied Jesus, but that wasn't really the case. Peter meant well, he loved the Lord passionately, but he didn't know better that the love of God cannot be expressed in the energy of the flesh. Like I said earlier, loyalty is a spiritual force and if you don't have the spirit in you, not even your biological relationship with someone can stop you from betraying him or her. There are two good examples: the case of Absalom revolting against his father and that of the brothers of Joseph selling him into slavery. Don't forget that disloyalty can come in the guise of envy, ambition or greed.

> Loyalty does not reduce people; it will only place you over those who think that you are being foolish or outdated serving a fellow man.

> Don't forget that disloyalty can come in the guise of envy, ambition or greed.

Chapter Nine: The Force Of Loyalty

The proof that Jesus understood Peter's situation perfectly was seen when He made him the head of the church after His resurrection.

A man who is self-centred cannot be loyal, because when he does he is only doing it because of what he stands to gain. I will say, without mincing words, that selfishness is the mother of disloyalty. Everybody loves a loyal person. Husbands love wives who are loyal and vice versa. Disloyalty can ruin any venture. Most pastors have suffered a church split because they were not discerning in their choice of people to hold very sensitive positions for them. Loyalty has to be tested and a confirmation from God must be obtained before you choose people for sensitive positions. If it required that you fast and pray fervently to get clearance from God, please do it!

> A man who is self-centred cannot be loyal, because when he does he is only doing it because of what he stands to gain.

> Selfishness is the mother of disloyalty.

In your search for loyal people you must be reminded again what loyalty is so as to help you in your search. To be loyal means to be faithful, firm in allegiance – to have a personal devotion to a sovereign government or a leader. You have to look for loyal people in your venture, because it is only then you can stand firm and tall. This is one of the secrets of success for most establishments.

> *Matthew 12:25*
> *...every kingdom divided against itself is brought to desolation; and every city or house divided against itself cannot stand.*

Do you know that Rahab's disloyalty to her nation finished the city of Jericho? The Christian world would not see anything wrong with what she did because her act favoured the nation of Israel. They are God's covenanted people, we would say. Can you imagine how her countrymen must have felt when, at the last minute, they discovered that Rahab had played a significant role in exposing their country and putting them in such jeopardy?

To enjoy favour with God and man, your absolute loyalty is demanded. God finished the people of Jericho by using a person who was disloyal among them. Following the simple law of logic, one of the tools God will most likely use when He wants to promote an establishment is a person who is loyal to His cause. God used Gamaliel to save the early Church from utter destruction when it came under intense persecution. This is because he was a notable voice among the religious leaders of his day.

In conclusion, let me add that loyalty is always demanded from subordinates, which should not always be the case. A boss needs to be loyal to those he is superior over, because without it he is bound not to enjoy favour with them too. We all need each other; just because you are a boss does not mean that you will not need the help of your juniors at work one way or another.

An Amalekite boss was not loyal to one of his subordinates and he paid dearly for it. On their way back from raiding Israel, one of the servants of this man, an Egyptian, became ill and was left behind. They may have left him to die, which to me was a display of callousness. David and his men met this abandoned man, took care of him and afterwards extracted useful information from him on how the Amalekites had raided Israel. He led David and his men to where the raiders were, thereby saving everyone they had taken hostage and getting back everything they had carted away with them. If his boss had been loyal to him he wouldn't have been caught in the first place. Be loyal to your boss, your colleagues and your subordinates. Read the story in 1 Samuel 30.

CHAPTER TEN

Favour Is A Seed

Matthew 5:7
Blessed are the merciful: for they shall obtain mercy.

If you want to enjoy favour for the rest of your life, you must learn to continually sow the seed of favour. Be nice and kind to people as much as possible. A lot of people want to be favoured, yet they will not show the slightest act of mercy to anyone they see in desperate need. Don't you know that what you sow you will reap?

> If you want to enjoy favour for the rest of your life, you must learn to continually sow the seed of favour.

Galatians 6:7
Be not deceived; God is not mocked: for whatsoever a man soweth, that shall he also reap.

There is a phenomenon that is now spreading that was almost rooted into my spirit, but for the mercy of God. Many have come under the belief that people will only repay good gestures with evil because of their ugly experiences of people under the spell of the end-time spirits. These days you may find out that those you tend to rely so much on end up stabbing you on the back. I would rather people attribute the bad treatment they get from others to the fact that they are dependent on people instead of God, or that they are casting their pearls before swine who end up repaying them evil for the good they've done. If anyone repays you evil for your goodness to him, leave such a one in God's hands. Let God deal with the person by Himself. The Scripture records, "Vengeance is mine; I will repay, says the Lord of Hosts." This should never make you stop being good, because that is the sole intention of the devil, since he knows that the principle of seedtime and harvest is the principle that runs the earth - Genesis 8:22.

I have had two nasty experiences of "big brothers" stealing from me. These were people I had helped in the past without any reservation. The most frightening was the case of the one who broke into my house. I found it horrifying and unbelievable. The good thing was that on both occasions, the Lord opened my eyes in the spirit to see them. And they couldn't deny it when I confronted them individually. In spite of God's mercy in revealing these acts to me, I discovered that I began to hold back from helping and showing kindness to people. My love began to grow cold, until I spent time on Galatians 6:7 quoted above.

The first thing that struck me was that I should not be deceived! I tell you also, do not be deceived. "Deceived by what?" you might ask me. I mean you should not be deceived by the experiences of the past when people repaid you evil for the good things you did for them. Do not be deceived that evil men are having the best while you are still languishing in lack. Do not be deceived that those who don't even pay tithes and give good offerings as much as you are living better. Do not be deceived that those brothers and sisters who sleep around, regardless of what the Word says, are living better. Perhaps you have now begun to compromise your own personal convictions.

Your situation cannot mock God for too long. What you sow you will reap. Have you shown any kind of favour in the past? Don't worry; you will reap that many times over. The condition, however, is in verse 9 of the same Galatians 6, "…you will reap if you faint not."

> Do not allow discouragement to rob you of your glorious inheritance in God.

Do not allow discouragement to rob you of your glorious inheritance in God. I do know, however, that the Bible says that the love of many shall wax cold in the last days because iniquity shall abound (Matthew 24:12). Regardless of that, Jesus still commands us to love one another and that brotherly love should continue (Hebrews 13:1). I must, at this junction, say that it is not as easy as I have described in this book.

Let me share this with you. After my graduation from university, I stayed home for some months without any employment. The major cause of the delay was my intention to travel out of Nigeria to make a living. Despite being very young in faith then, I was still able to know that it was not God's will for me at that time. I soft-pedalled on my efforts and decided to stay in Nigeria and practise my profession. Because I was not ready to obey God fully, I never really took the job issue seriously. I prayed for a job, but not as fervently as I usually would have handled other serious issues.

One morning after my devotions, I heard sharply in my spirit, "When you were planning your overseas trip, you fasted and prayed, but now that I have told you to stay and take a job, you never bother to fast and pray for it. Why?"

I knew immediately that it was the Lord speaking to me. And so I replied and said, "Lord, I fasted."

I heard again, "No, you never did!"

I replied again, saying that I did.

After the third query from the Spirit of God, I told Him that I was very sorry for arguing with Him. As soon as I accepted that I hadn't fasted about the job issue, He then spoke to me, "I know you fast and pray, but which of the fasts did you specifically dedicate to your job?"

"Oh, I see." My eyes lit up with realisation. "I have already had my breakfast this morning, but starting from tomorrow, I will go into three days' fasting and prayers to seek your face on it."

On the first day of the fast, in a vision of the night as brother Novel Hayes would call it, I saw a dwarf holding two offers of employment in his hands. I snatched one of them and told him that I couldn't be jobless and let him have two offers of employment. This dwarf ran after me everywhere I went, trying to snatch back the letter, but I wouldn't let him. All of a sudden I saw the two of us in the clouds. He was reporting me to a being whose face I couldn't see. This tiny devil spoke all manner of things against me in that vision.

After his speech, I heard a baritone voice from the cloud saying, "What have you to say to all these things he has said against you?"

All I could reply was, "I am a generous man." As soon as I said that, a portion of the clouds cleared and I saw a guy whom I had helped in 1985. Before I could ask the One who told me to defend myself to ask the guy if I hadn't helped him before, the clouds moved back into position and I came back to consciousness. I had helped this guy with a pair of nice trainers that an in-law had given to me. He had asked me for them after I finished my secondary school final examinations and was preparing to go home. I never wanted to give them to him, but since he persisted, I gave the trainers to him and never thought about it again. God saw that even though the pair of trainers was like an idol to me, I released them all the same from my heart.

On the second day of the fast, the Lord visited me again and showed me the company I was to work for. I shared this revelation with my then host and it came to pass exactly the way God had revealed it to me. Halleluiah! It pays to do well. Imagine a pair of trainers - a used pair of trainers for that matter. They were now being used as a platform of reckoning for a good multinational job. The vision showed that they were in my record in heaven and that they opened up a job opportunity for me eight years later. I worked in that establishment for close to a decade before resigning for the greater assignment of the gospel work I am now doing.

It is my earnest prayer that your faith will be strengthened again unto good works. You see, heaven and earth may pass away, but not a jot of God's word will remain unfulfilled. That someone has disappointed you before is not an indication that you will not reap all the acts of favour you have shown in the past. The person might just have sown an evil seed, which, according to the principles of life and living, must produce a commensurate harvest for him and may not have anything to do with your own expected harvest.

Joseph was hated by his brothers and sold into slavery, he went to prison for a rape he never committed, yet all those experiences were not strong enough to truncate the will of God for his life.

Favour is God's will and none of the nasty, heart-breaking experiences you are having today will stop your harvest in Jesus' name.

Mordecai saved the life of King Ahasuerus of Shushan the great when two of the king's eunuchs made a plot to kill him. Mordecai knew about the plot by the two guards and foiled it, thereby saving the king's life. This was an act of favour by Mordecai, a seed sown in the king's life. But it was not too long before Mordecai himself was in trouble. Haman, an enemy of the Jews, was planning to kill him because there was a personality clash between them. Mordecai would not bow to greet Haman the way others did because the Jews don't bow to men, just God, and this injured Haman's ego in no small measure. Since life runs on the principle of seedtime and harvest, God denied the king his sleep, a night before Haman planned to strike Mordecai and the entire Jewish race embodied in Shushan the great. A book of remembrance was opened to reward the man who saved the king's life, thereby transferring to Haman's head the death sentence meant for Mordecai. Read the book of Esther to enjoy this beautiful story of God's power to save in difficult times.

We should not allow the devil to deceive us away from being good, because seedtime and harvest still exist.

Some years back, a sister in Christ and a friend of mine told me a story I will never forget. It was a true story of how God lifted a woman from grass to grace on the platform of the good seeds she had sown in the lives of many who came her way. My friend told me how she had paid this woman a visit in her struggling days and didn't like what she met that particular day. A creditor had come to ask this woman to pay what she owed him or she would be disgraced. True to the creditor's threat, it became an unpleasant scene that no one would pray to experience because of all that he did to this woman. According to my friend, what came out of this woman's mouth to her after the creditor had finished his one-man soap opera was, "Have you eaten?" She said that she couldn't believe that the woman could still give free food to anyone, in a business where she struggled with debts. How many of us could truly do that? But today, the story has changed: this woman has built houses, sent some of her children abroad to study and drives good cars. She has become a notable name in the catering business. My friend didn't just tell this story because she loves to talk. She told me because of the question I asked the day that both of us went to eat in that restaurant. It was when I wondered why people were trooping into the restaurant that she decided to tell me the little she knew about the woman's generosity that has paid off tremendously today. It is indeed true that there is no glory without a story.

Say these words: Devil! In the name of Jesus Christ of Nazareth, I refuse to believe that I will reap evil for all the good things the Lord has used me to do in the lives of others. It is a lie from you and your hosts, orchestrated to rob me of my blessings by the distortion of my good expectations. I will always reap in mercy because I sow in righteousness. I am blessed and highly favoured. Everything is working for good no matter how dark it appears today. It is superlatively well with me.

CHAPTER ELEVEN

Releasing Favour By Warfare

You can release favour by warfare. A preacher once said that it was unnecessary to pray for favour because God through Christ already favours us. I don't quite agree with him, because the Bible says, "ye have not because ye ask not" - James 4:2. For God to have said that we do not have because we do not ask definitely means that the thing He expects us to ask for is covered in His will for us. We all know that by the stripes of Jesus Christ of Nazareth we have been made whole already, but people still come onto healing lines to be prayed for. Health is a finished work, I know, but we must establish it when we feel sick because there will always be forces out there to discredit the goodness of the Lord in the hearts of us, His precious Saints. Favour, like any other will of God for our lives, therefore demands that we ask for it before we can enjoy it.

Psalm 106:4-5
Remember me, O LORD, with the favour that thou bearest unto thy people: visit me with thy salvation; that I may see the good of thy chosen, that I may rejoice in the gladness of thy nation, that I may glory in thy inheritance.

Like I said earlier, has Christ not paid for our sicknesses and diseases? Why, then, do we still have sick folks today? Or better put, why do we pray for sick folks in our churches today? A lot of people are sick because of sheer ignorance, passivity towards the issue of divine healing or possibly because they are under attack from Satan to test if they believe what they profess about healing. What the preacher should have said is that the believer should not beg for favour because it has been purchased already through Christ Jesus. When you are not seeing its traces or the reverse is what you are experiencing, I urge you in the name of Jesus to brace up and put your prayer garments on to enforce it. Fight until favour begins to flow like an ocean to you everywhere you go. Here's the flipside to this issue: if you do not show

> **If you do not show favour to other people, then don't expect that favour will be released to you no matter how much you fight.**

favour to other people, then don't expect that favour will be released to you no matter how much you fight.

Christianity is a matter of faith and so we cannot afford to be at ease at all. Our faith is the victory that overcomes the world and no one can overcome without a confrontation with demoniacal forces, which will always attempt to disprove the efficacy of the Word of God. You must always remember that Satan and his hosts want you down as much as possible. They want your home destroyed, your businesses grounded and your health in jeopardy. They want everything about you to be nothing to write home about. Nothing can cause stagnation for a man like dwelling in the successes of yesteryear. At no time should anybody think that he has everything there is to get or that he has achieved everything there is to achieve, because life is always progressive. God did not design life to be stagnant at any time; that is why when we have nothing to add, we start reducing from that moment onward. Peter thought that everything there was to following Jesus was the transfiguration experience. He wanted to build a monument around that experience, not knowing that the death, burial and resurrection of Jesus Christ and even the birth of the Church were still events that would be unfolded in his lifetime.

You must keep increasing until you finish your assignment here on earth. There are so many people who cannot explain the reason for the seeming absence of God's favour from their lives. They just feel that the favour of God is no longer as strong around them as it used to be. Perhaps these few words from a great woman of God, Joyce Meyer, will give you an insight. She says, "Every new level attracts new devils to contend with."

Why would new devils confront you? They are there to either dethrone you or stop you from making any further progress in your walk with God. As long as His fire is still burning as strongly around you, His favour will be very potent to help you sail through every challenge.

You can increase God's favour around you by waging war against the enemy in order to gain access to what rightfully belongs to you. There may be demon spirits hindering the manifestation of God's favour in the area of your expected promotion or in your bid to purchase a car or buy a home of your dream. The problem is not with God; rather, it is with you. This is because His faithfulness forbids Him from failing to keep His part of the deal. Just like in Daniel's case, answers to his prayers had been released twenty-one days before he received them in the place of persistent prayers. God is vindicated when we discover that it is demon spirits and not Him that is responsible for the delay.

I think it is pitiful to hear any brother say that in the past he used to pray for six hours at a stretch but now only manages to recite Psalms 23, or the Lord's Prayer as it is called. A brother was recollecting how hot he used to be and said something like this: "Oh, I remember when I used to be on fire for God; that was when Christianity was still Christianity." The simple question I asked in my heart was, "Has Christianity now become Islam?" Christianity has not changed; it is people who have shifted in their zeal for God. We must wake up and take our destiny by force, because our adversary the devil is not a gentle person at all. He is wickedness personified.

Jabez never enjoyed favour with God and man in the

initial stages of his life. Only God could tell what informed the terrible woes that followed him everywhere he went. I believe that he first thought that everything happening around him was natural until the unthinkable happened to convince him that he had to cry out to God for help. Before the Bible gives us the account that he became more honourable than all his brethren, we can deduce that he was not in any way comparable to any of them. If not, it would not be sufficient news for any of us to anchor our faith upon seeking positive changes in the issues confronting us today. Through warfare Jabez became more favoured than any of the brethren. You can pray for favour. It is part of your redemptive benefits.

> Through warfare Jabez became more favoured than any of the brethren.

One of my spiritual sons in the Lord followed me home one evening after a Wednesday bible study. The look on his face showed that something was definitely wrong with him. He explained his ordeal when we got home. He had lost his mechanic workshop a few months before, thereby losing virtually all his customers when he moved to a new place. After six months in the new place his business was almost non-existent. He became bankrupt and couldn't pay his rent, which was due then. Someone advised him to erect a bigger sign to help direct new customers to his workshop, which he did. The painful thing was that barely an hour after he erected the sign, the local authorities came calling. He was made to pay a whole year's charges for the sign because they wouldn't believe that he had put it up just an hour before. He had to borrow money to avoid being taken to court. He got very fed up and discouraged when he explained all his troubles to me that night. He concluded that God had forsaken him. I immediately knew what was wrong, because the Spirit impressed upon my heart that we needed to make wars in the spirit to establish him in his new place. "It is a spiritual sign you need," I said. We went into three days of fasting and prayer to change the situation and enforce the favour of God upon his life and business.

The very first day of the fasting and prayer, the problem was revealed. A woman appeared to him in his dream and told him that she was the one behind all his troubles in Lagos and that things would not change whether or not we prayed and fasted. I knew that the Lord wanted us to know where the arrows were coming from. We destroyed the works of the devil through this woman and things changed drastically for him. From the second day vehicles had started rolling in, but I told him that we must finish the three days we promised the Lord before he could resume work. You too can make wars in the spirit to get things moving.

I will share my own experience as well. I had invested some money into buying cars and other items for sale just before I went into the full-time ministry. There was one particular car that nobody wanted to buy. I displayed it for eight months from one notable showroom to the other, but it wouldn't just sell. I went to a prayer camp to know why it wouldn't sell, at whatever level it was priced. What I saw in the spirit after my time out to pray baffled me. Two of the tyres had been removed and replaced with blocks and there was dust all over the car, to the extent that you wouldn't know that it was close to new. I commanded that the tyres be replaced and the dust be wiped by the blood of Jesus Christ. Guess what? The very first contact I made after I came back from camp took me to the man who bought the car. Praise God. You can secure favour by warfare.

The Psalmist prayed and put God in remembrance of certain things. He said that God should remember him with the favour reserved for the people of God. That means that he knew that there was "the favour" for the people of God. It is not just any kind of favour. It is _the_ favour. It is definite! My son in the Lord had customers reserved for him, but warfare brought them about. I had the buyer reserved to buy my car that was tied down for eight months, but warfare connected us.

> Nobody will tamper with a reserved seat if he sees there is already a name on it.

> The knowledge of the fact that you are a candidate for God's favour gives you the boldness to take it by force.

This kind of favour has the power to raise the dead, cause the lame to walk and make blind eyes see. It is superior to any manmade favour. It is the favour reserved. It is always there. It is not something that you begin to manufacture during an emergency. It is reserved! Nobody will tamper with a reserved seat if he sees there is already a name on it. Isn't that the case? You can fight for it if you meet anyone sitting on it. Why? Because you know you are not guessing. Your name is on it. In the same way, you have read the Bible and have seen in its pages that there is _the_ favour of health, fruitfulness, promotion, wealth, long life, peace, joy and so on for you to wage war for. The knowledge of the fact that you are a candidate for God's favour gives you the boldness to take it by force.

Say these words after me: *There is "the favour" reserved for me, I know it! Therefore Satan, I command you to loose your hold of it in the name of Jesus Christ of Nazareth. I destroy everything you have used as a veil to cover my eyes from seeing it. I pull down every spiritual obstacle hindering the manifestation. I command the free flow of the favour reserved for me from today. I am the healed because it is reserved for me by the stripes of Jesus. I am the prosperous one because wealth, riches and honour are reserved for me. I am the lifted one because there is an enviable position reserved at the top for me. I enjoy supernatural favour everywhere I go. I have a reservation where kings and princes gather to dine in every place the Lord leads me to. I am treated honourably and royally because I am God's ambassador to nations in Christ Jesus. I am always celebrated and not tolerated. I am above only in Jesus' name – amen. Halleluiah!*

CHAPTER TWELVE

The Force Of Hardwork

> If in God's favour we have life, then outside of it is death, by the simple law of logic.

We often hear the phrase, "There is no food for the lazy man." Nothing can be truer. This is because the Bible categorically states that whoever will not work should not eat. If in God's favour we have life, then outside of it is death, by the simple law of logic - Psalm 30:5. That means that laziness and death are synonymous, since lack of work will deny us food that helps the physical life.

In Genesis 2:15, God told Adam to dress and keep the Garden of Eden. The word "dress" simply means "value addition". That means that every one of God's assignments for each man is for value addition. Teachers add value to society by providing education. The police help enforce law and order. Bus and truck drivers add value to society by moving people and things from one place to the other. Builders help keep us from being homeless. God-ordained work is for value addition. That is why we enjoy the favour of our employers by way of the wages they pay us. You only pay those who are on your payroll. On the other hand, there are those

> God-ordained work is for value addition.

who fall out of favour with the government and society at large because of the kind of work they do - it destroys value. Can you imagine the nuisance those on drugs pose to the government and the homes they come from? This means that people who sell drugs or those involved in armed robbery destroy value because they cause great pain, not just to their victims but also to their friends and family members.

I know that we should work very hard on our jobs, but the first thing is that we ought to know the kind of job in which we should work very hard. For instance, the Bible says that those who are in the habit of stealing should desist from it. We are not to continue in evil.

Ephesians 4:28
Let him that stole steal no more: but rather let him labour, working with his hands the thing which is good, that he may have to give to him that needeth.

Every man was born with a purpose. And with that purpose comes certain natural gifts that are to help enhance the purpose. Therefore, to enjoy favour in our jobs it is good that we first locate what we are created for. This is because buried in every purpose is the wisdom to fulfil it. Michael Jackson seemed always to know the kind of dance steps that create lasting effects in people's minds. Mohammed Ali knew when and where to give an uppercut that threw his opponents off balance to make him one of the greatest in boxing history. But the same Ali would probably have not sold a thousand copies if he had released a music album.

These two guys did not become great because they were the most hard-working guys around, but because they knew their areas of gift and worked very hard at developing them. For instance, Michael Jackson in his life time had the problem of people wanting to catch a glimpse of him, or if possible touch him or ask him to sign an autograph. That to me is favour. Come to think of it, can you deny a person you adore a thing they ask you for if you really have the wherewithal to give it? Arnold Schwarzenegger was Governor of California because his gift made room for him. His popularity and acceptance level soared because of his acting skills.

Chapter Twelve: The Force Of Hardwork

Hollywood and the other constituent parts of California could not resist him at the time.

It was not until I watched Kirk Franklin live for the first time in London in 2000 that I realised how much perfection these stars bring to their work. I began to appreciate the fact that a live show cannot be compared to a music video. If I had a million dollars that day, I would not have hesitated one bit to give some of it to him in addition to the wealth he already has.

You can see favour at work in all the people I have mentioned. Come to think of it, if someone gifted in tailoring goes into building because he thinks that there are better prospects for him there, do you think that he will last in that job without serving a sentence for risking people's lives? Rather than being mentioned as an example of excellence in his area of expertise, he will be berated and hounded for his mediocrity. Stay in your area of strength, because it will overshadow your areas of weakness. That is why most people want to marry superstars. It is not just for the fame or money but because an area of perfection is being projected.

> Stay in your area of strength, because it will overshadow your areas of weakness.

Without hard work, favour is not in view. This is because nobody likes a lazy person. As a former operations manager in a manufacturing company, I know the kind of fever that often gripped workers any time there was going to be a restructuring. Those who knew that they had not measured up, even by their own reckoning, used to have the worst of times. Their guesses were always accurate, because they would be relieved of their jobs to give room to those who were committed to the vision of the company. It was always a very bad time for those with poor appraisals in the year under review. Those who knew that they had done very well bounced up and down, while those who knew that they had done badly always started the funeral before the death of their jobs.

One has to know the background of my country to appreciate what I am saying. Nigeria is not like an advanced country where you can get social support when you are out of a job. There is nothing like that. And so when one is out, one is out. The second thing is that getting employment is not a stroll in the park. In the UK, for instance, there are short-term contracts you can easily get to keep body and soul together while you wait to hit the big one. But in my country, you can spend close to six years searching for work to no avail. The fact is that despite people knowing how tough it is getting a job, they still toy with it when they have it. Can you see how hard work affects the degree of favour one stands to enjoy with God and with man?

I advise that people should replace employment with employability. When you seek after employability, you will be sought after sooner or later. Employability demands that you are not only hard working, but also very knowledgeable in your job. Your thorough knowledge of your job should be second to none. It also demands that you are versatile. For instance, I will readily employ someone with both accounting and administrative skills as against someone who is only good at accounting. Better still, I will prefer someone who has IT skills in addition to the first two. But it will take someone who really is a hard worker to be qualified in all the fields I have mentioned.

> When you seek after employability, you will be sought after sooner or later.

I do know that the race does not go to the swift, nor the battle to the strong. But our faith in God is no

> Our faith in God is no substitute for hard work.

substitute for hard work, no matter how great it is. The church today has used the word grace as a substitute for mediocrity. When a brother or sister tells you that he or she would attend a function by God's grace, they mean, indirectly, that they will not be found there. When they really want to come, they say it in the affirmative and you're sure to find them there. This is a great irony. The grace of God is being equated with inability and floppiness. But the truth is that grace is not inability but a divine ability that helps one to do the impossible.

CHAPTER THIRTEEN

Love, The Greatest Of All

Love is the greatest of all. When faith, hope and love were paraded, love stole the show in 1 Corinthians 13:13. Without faith it is impossible to please God. I know. But don't forget that faith does not work alone. Faith works by love. So love is still the determinant of the fate of the faith that you see anyone exercising.

Jesus declared love to be the greatest of all the commandments when a scribe asked Him which was the greatest of them all. Like a man of God said, "Using the law of logic, the greatest of the blessings of God are released when His greatest commandment is obeyed." Nothing provokes the favour of God like love. When Paul and Silas were thrown into the Philippian jail, love moved them into singing and praising God in spite of all the bruises sustained in

> Using the law of logic, the greatest of the blessings of God are released when His greatest commandment is obeyed.

the course of preaching Christ. Do you know that the one you love you hate to offend? They gullibly obeyed what the Word says: "in all things give thanks…" Their action moved God to organise their freedom. In one of my messages titled "The great earthquake", I explained that the greatness of the earthquake was not in the catastrophic effect it had when it occurred, but in the history it made by singling out just one building, which happened to be where Paul and Silas were being kept. The earthquake delivered them. I know earthquakes as destructive occurrences, but glory to God because for Paul and Silas it was the earthquake of freedom. The earthquake that had the keys to all the prison doors had to be a great one. The earthquake that never sank or caused the prison house to collapse had to be great. The earthquake that kept the prison guard asleep until all the doors had been opened had to be a great one. Please help me give God praise, halleluiah!

> Paul and Silas showed their love for God through the prayer and praise jamboree they had in the prison.

Don't let us forget what Jesus Christ said while on His mission on earth. He said that the proof of anyone's love for Him is in obedience to His commandments. Paul and Silas showed their love for God through the prayer and praise jamboree they had in the prison. And the favour of deliverance was wrought for them. Remember that deliverance from harm and the intentions of the enemy is one of the proofs of God's favour upon a life (Psalm 41:11).

John 14:21
He that hath my commandments, and keepeth them, he it is that loveth me: and he that loveth me shall be loved of my Father, and I will love him, and I will manifest myself to him.

What we need the most, as children of God, is love, which unfortunately is scarce in these last days. Jesus prophesied that the enemy would use his multiplied evils to weaken the force of love (Matthew 24:12). And is it not happening before our very eyes? We can hardly trust each other any more. Pastors and their assistants watch each other's back night and day as if there is anything more to soul winning than the expansion of the Kingdom of Our great and mighty God. Two things split churches now: arguments over money and strife over who is more favoured and accepted among the innocent parishioners (who sometimes are undiscerning pawns in the hands of ambitious men and women who have lost touch with God). I keep telling folks who are close to me: "I don't need an experienced man of God to be with, all I desire passionately is a current man of God who can tell me without gainsaying, 'Thus saith the Lord.'" That was the difference between the old prophet and the young in 1 Kings 13. The old prophet was experienced but the young was current. The young prophet who was at the cutting edge of his mandate at the time allowed the experienced prophet to use the supposed voice of an angel he heard to mess up his life.

Who talks about the power to heal the sick or raise the dead any more when all we are preoccupied with is who is better in homiletics and eloquence? I have often thought that Apostle Paul would weep if he rose from the dead to see what the church has now become in comparison to the passion he had for the gospel when he wrote, "For me to live is Christ, to die is gain." Or "I am crucified with Christ and the life I now live is not mine but that of the Son of God." Or "Woe is me if I preach not the gospel." The woe he was alluding to had nothing to do with having to forfeit his honorarium if he didn't preach, or that he would not be aired on TBN or GOD CHANNEL. He meant that he wouldn't be fulfilled if

Chapter Thirteen: Love, The Greatest Of All

he did not do the one thing he had been called to do - the only thing worth living for.

Most of us talk about the fiery revelations of God through the words of Paul as if to say, well, he didn't quite do as much as we tend to project his achievements. The truth of the matter is that he excelled with God's revelation plus his personal dedication. Was it a revelation to say "Woe is me if I preach not the gospel" or a personal decision borne out of his encounter with Christ? Was it a revelation when he said "I have learnt to abase and abound" or was it his resolution to be totally committed to God and His Christ?

The preaching of holiness is not the answer to holy living; the love of Jesus is. It is the revelation how much of His unfailing love He showers on us on a daily basis in spite of our shortcomings that makes us want to please Him. Do you know that hatred hardens people and helps to boost rebellion? It is very difficult to work against someone you know truly loves you, except if that love is not known to you yet. From the scriptural verse

> The preaching of holiness is not the answer to holy living; the love of Jesus is.

> It is very difficult to work against someone you know truly loves you, except if that love is not known to you yet.

above, we can see that it is the love of God that makes us obey Him. And that is the only way God Himself can be fulfilled – when we act in obedience. This is because He is not a tyrant; everything He warns us against is for our own good, not His.

You cannot love your neighbour unless it is first settled in your heart that God loves you. Just like we know that the moon has no light of its own, so no man has any love of his own to give. It is the reflection of the light from the sun that gives the moon its light. Therefore we can thankfully conclude that the love of God that is beamed into us by the Holy Spirit is what helps us love our neighbours. People want to rebel against God every time they cannot see Him representing their interest. But what we must realise is that God's love is not manifested only when we buy a new house or when we get promoted in our job. We should also see His love when He tells us to desist from habits capable of destroying or shortening our lives.

A super salesman once said that the product that has made the most significant impact on your life is the

Chapter Thirteen: Love, The Greatest Of All

product that you can easily sell. This is because the evidence of the product will be undeniable when showing customers what it has done for you. If you have not experienced or acknowledged God's love, it will be difficult to advertise it by way of living it for all to see and admire. The rebellion of the children of Israel was borne out of the deception that the challenges they encountered were an indication that God didn't love them. Hence, they could not love Him back to obey Him and provoke His favour.

> A super salesman once said that the product that has made the most significant impact on your life is the product that you can easily sell.

Deuteronomy 1:27
And ye murmured in your tents, and said, because the LORD hated us, he hath brought us forth out of the land of Egypt, to deliver us into the hand of the Amorites, to destroy us.

If God tells you not to do Internet or credit card deals now that you are born again, or if He tells you that you should stop prostituting your body for a living, don't see it as an act of His hatred for you, to deny you riches, but

His hatred for seeing you ending up in jail. See it as an act of His hatred to see you die of any of the venereal diseases around today. It is only when this simple fact is in place that obeying God becomes a thing of joy and not a thing to be sorrowful about.

Love provokes the favour of God more than anything. A Muslim convert had this to tell me when we were on our way to pray for his sick daughter: "I am from a staunch Muslim home. My wife's parents and mine are serious scholars in the Islamic faith. I got converted on the naming ceremony of my first son. My elder brother's wife, who is equally a convert, had brought members of her church to pray for the baby. She had intended that after the Islamic rites were done with, the church folks could come in and say their prayers. On sighting the Christian group, the whole atmosphere changed. The gathering began to sing and say things against the Christian faith capable of causing a rift between both faiths. I had thought my child's naming ceremony had been messed up, in the hope that the Christians would join issues with the disparaging Muslims. However, the Christians defeated any such expectations. When my Muslim folks had finished and it was time for the Christians to say their prayers, all I was waiting to hear was a counter to all that had been said against them. To my amazement the Christians said their prayers and left without replying to any of the provocative words said by my Muslim folks. When my wife and I went to bed that night, I said to her that I wasn't going to be a Muslim any longer. I told her that I was going for a change of faith. I explained to her what had informed my decision: that it was the good conduct the Christians had displayed by not replying to all that was said against them that won my heart. My wife never hesitated one bit in declaring her solidarity. She changed straight away and we have since been waxing very strong in our new-found faith. The Christians were full of love that was real and genuine," he concluded.

Can you see the power of God's agape love and what it is capable of doing? It provokes the favour of God and man. It melted the hearts of two former Muslims who are now burning with fervour for the Lord. Even though they do not attend the church where I pastor, we have become very good friends since. They came over to be filled with the Holy Spirit recently and, glory to God, they had an overdose of Him and spoke in tongues powerfully.

> **You are losing when you do not love.**

You are losing when you do not love. That is the candid truth. Love covers a multitude of sins. So the more you help those struggling to stand on their feet, the more they will love and appreciate you. It is only then that you can get through to help them stand up and be the best for God and for themselves. Some think that their spirituality can be measured by how much criticism they mete out to wrongdoers. This is far from the truth. I do agree that we should rebuke people when we see them doing wrong things. But this must be done in the spirit of love and meekness. If not, we will succeed in hardening them and jeopardising what we are out to achieve.

> **Love does not wait for what it can get before expressing itself; it expresses itself because it knows that will bring what it wants.**

Love is not haughty. Love is not envious. Love is not greedy for gain, in other words it is not there only for what it can get but for what it can give. Love is considerate. Love is not destructive. Love is life. Above all, God is Love.

Love does not wait for what it can

get before expressing itself; it expresses itself because it knows that will bring what it wants. Love gave us Jesus Christ in spite of the failure of the human race. That was the way God could reach out to us. And praise God it worked, because that is why you and I are children of the Most High God today. That is why this book is in your hands.

John 3:16
For God so loved the world, that he gave his only begotten Son, that whosoever believeth in him should not perish, but have everlasting life.

Romans 5:8
But God commendeth his love toward us, in that while we were yet sinners, Christ died for us.

John 15:13
Greater love hath no man than this, that a man lay down his life for his friends.

GOD'S LOVE WILL BRING FAVOUR YOUR WAY.

Nothing works against a man working in the agape love of God. He may be killed and buried but since love never dies, he will rise again. Some have stopped giving because people often repay them with evil; go on with your good works, because if you don't faint in your love's work you will reap abundance very soon.

Romans 8:29
And we know that all things work together for good to them that love God, to them who are the called according to his purpose.

> **The love you show to your fellow man is the only proof of your love for God.**

A point of correction here: if you claim to love God whom you have not seen and you do not love your neighbour whom you see daily, you are deceiving yourself. The love you show to your fellow man is the only proof of your love for God.

The love of God guarantees God's great deliverances when in danger. It gives divine promotions and honour in every endeavour. Above all, it guarantees good health and longevity.

Psalm 91:14-16
Because he has set his love upon me, therefore will I deliver him: I will set him on high, because he hath known my name. He shall call upon me, and I will answer him: I will be with him in trouble; I will deliver him, and honour him. With long life will I satisfy him, and shew him my salvation

ABOUT THE AUTHOR

Oluwole Adekunle is senior pastor of the Reality of Grace Ministries International, a vibrant multicultural church located south east of the London metropolis. A mechanical engineer by profession, he worked as an operations manager in the food drinks unit of one of Nigeria's largest food and beverage multinational companies before resigning to answer the call of God in his life.

Pastor Olu is an entrepreneur, a psalmist with a 12-track debut album titled TIMELESS GOSPEL released in 2010, and an author with three life-transforming books to his credit – *Your Words Shape Your World*, *Provoking God's Favour* and *Prosperity without Tears* – all by the grace of God.

He teaches the Word with simplicity and practicality, making it easy for both comprehension and application. Pastor Olu is a man of signs and wonders through the operation of the gifts of the Spirit. His popular weekly telecast *Grace Time Today* runs across Europe, Africa and the Far East, blessing millions of viewers. His teachings are available in audio and video formats.

BOOKS BY OLUWOLE ADEKUNLE

Your words Shape Your World
Prosperity Without Tears
Provoking God's Favour